Copyright © 2025

All rights reserved. No part of this publication may be reproduced, distributed, or transmitted in any form or by any means without the prior written permission of the author All Wikimedia images are in the public domain.

Except the work by Emily Tjonmsland, Christ,
which was used by permission.

Dedication

This Book is dedicated to

the One about whom the Volume of the Book speaks,

the Lord Jesus Christ. May His family grow.

In memory of Charlie Kirk

Acknowledgements

My humble gratitude for the inspiration of the Holy Spirit who guided this work.
To my wonderful wife, Telli, whose love and support helped me finish this project through many health concerns.
To family, those who encouraged me and those lost in hatred and spite. May they be found.
To Pastor Charlie whose passion for the Word of God, in-depth study of the original Hebrew, and comprehensive commentaries ensured the theological soundness of this work, despite his own health concerns, pastoral duties, and struggles with hurricanes and Chihuahuas.
To Emily Tjonmsland, whose masterful work of Christ graces the cover.
To all the gifted artists, past and present, whose inclusion in this work help us connect to the individuals and events recorded in Scripture.

Cover: Christ by Emily Tjonmsland (2024)
Scripture in Italics – guided by the English Standard Version

Forward

This collection of sacred art and reflection invites you into the Bible's grand narrative, where each brushstroke and biblical scene reveals the unfolding story of God's love for humanity. The paintings, rich in beauty and symbolism, capture pivotal moments from Scripture, while the accompanying explanations illuminate their place in the divine tapestry of salvation. Woven throughout is the thread of Jesus Christ, the promised Redeemer, whose life, death, and resurrection fulfill the ancient prophecies, and which give meaning to every page. May this book draw you closer to the heart of God's redemptive plan, as you see His Son reflected in both image and word.

                        Emlen S. "Charlie" Garrett
                        Pastor, The Superior Word
                            Sarasota, Florida

Forgiven

Christ and the Penitent Sinners by Pieter Paul Rubens (1618)

Preface

The story of human existence began thousands of years ago and recorded in Scripture for those searching for the meaning of life. Some, however, are veiled (2 Corinthians 3), others live in darkness.

The complete story provides clarity. It is about One individual whose sacrifice opened the way for reconciliation with His creation. However, some do not want you to hear or understand.

Warning—*We wrestle not against flesh and blood, but against the rulers, against the authorities, against the cosmic powers over this present darkness, against the spiritual forces of evil in the heavenly places.* (Ephesians 6:12)

Table of Contents

Dedication i	Abimelech 50
Acknowledgements ii	Abraham's Sacrifice 52
Forward iii	Finding a Bride 54
Preface v	The Effect of Beauty 56
Creator 2	Isaac's Blessing 58
John the Apostle 4	Bridge between Heaven and Earth 60
Paul the Apostle 6	Good from Evil 62
Naming the Animals 8	The Lord with Jacob 64
The Lord with Adam and Eve in the Garden 10	Reconciliation 66
The First Deception 12	Rape of Dinah 68
Seed of the Woman 14	Death of Rachel 70
The Acceptable Sacrifice 16	Dreams 72
The Lord Speaks to Cain 18	Rejected by His Brothers 74
Enoch Translated 20	Jacob Mourns His Son 76
Gospel Message 22	Judah and Tamar 78
The Deluge 24	Potiphar's Wife 80
Clean and Unclean Animals 26	Interpreting Dreams 82
Renewing the World 28	Pharaoh's Signet Ring 84
The Lord Saves Noah 30	Joseph 86
God's Covenant with Noah 32	Double Portion 88
Tower of Babel 34	Jacob blesses His Sons 90
The Call of Abraham 36	The Suffering of Job 92
Melchizedek 38	Saved from the Waters 94
God's Covenant with Abraham 40	Feeding the Sheep 96
The Angel of the Lord with Hagar 42	I AM 98
Abrahamic Covenant 44	Ten Plagues on Egypt 100
The Lord Visits Abraham 46	Passover 102
Sodom and Gomorrah 48	The Pain of Loss 104

Pillar of Light	106
Crossing the Red Sea	108
The People were Protected	110
Manna	112
The Blessing	114
Land of Milk and Honey	116
Moses and the Rock	118
The Fight with Amalek	120
Receiving the Law	122
Outrage	124
Tabernacle	126
Ark of the Covenant	128
Brass Serpent	130
The Angel of the Lord with Balaam and his Donkey	132
Seduction	134
Unauthorized Fire	136
Daughters of Zelophehad	138
Cities of Refuge	140
Cleansing a House	142
Levitical Sacrifices	144
Substitution	146
Death of Moses	148
Rahab	150
The Lord with Joshua	152
Taking Jericho	154
Sun Stands Still	156
Ehud	158
Deborah	160
The Lord with Gideon	162
Jephthah	164
Foretelling the Birth of Samson	166
Samson	168
Samson and Deliah – Betrayal	170
Samson's Death	172
How Far can Men Fall	174
Return to Bethlehem	176
Goel	178
Hannah Prays for a Son	180
The Lord Speaks to Samuel	182
Ark Taken	184
Saul as King	186
Anointing David	188
Playing for the King	190
David and Goliath	192
Abigail	194
The Witch of Endor	196
Death of Saul	198
Return of the Ark of the Covenant	200
Rebuke, Humbleness, Forgiveness	202
David's Census Brings Pestilence	204
Absalom's Death	206
Succession	208
My Servant	210
The Lord Grants Solomon Wisdom	212
The Judgement of Solomon – Sacrifice	214
Solomon's Temple	216
All is Vanity	218
The King's Love	220
Sad Ending	222

Division of the Kingdom	224
Consequences of Idolatry	226
Raised from the Dead	228
Accepting the Sacrifice	230
Power of God Came Upon Him	232
The Angel of the Lord with Elijah	234
Naboth's Vineyard	236
Elijah's Ascension	238
Dividing the Waters	240
Healing the Stew	242
Namaan's Healing	244
Queen Athaliah – King Joash	246
Raised from the Dead	248
Immanuel	250
Cast Down	252
Leviathan	254
Healing the Blind	256
Healing the Lame	258
The Angel of the Lord Destroys the Assyrians	260
Sent	262
Speaking Plainly	264
King Manasseh	266
The Last Good King	268
The Scribe	270
Babylonian Captivity	274
The Mission	276
Gospel Message	278
The Glory of the Lord	280
Valley of Dry Bones	282
Gog	284
Kingdoms of the World	286
The Fiery Furnace	288
Handwriting on the Wall	290
Daniel in the Lions' Den	292
Endtime Prophecy	294
Return	296
Esther	298
Bethlehem	300
Gabriel visits Zechariah	302
Massacre of the Innocents	304
Out of Egypt I called My Son	306
Vision of Four Chariots	308
He is Coming	310
Feast of Tabernacles	312
The King Riding a Donkey	314
Unleavened Bread	316
Requirement for Return	318
The Great Day of the Lord's Wrath	320
Meaning behind the letters	322
The Road to Emmaus	324
Shroud of Turin	326
Indwelling Spirit	328
Illustrations and Art	330
Editor	339

Christ in the Old Testament

Creator
Genesis 1

The Ancient of Days by William Blake (1794)

In Scripture, a two-letter Hebrew word, *"eth,"* appears about seven thousand times and is usually left untranslated because it functions as the accusative marker in sentences. It is composed of the Hebrew letters alef and tav.

It is found in the first verse (see Preface) following the word Elohim, which reads *"In the beginning created God **alef-tav** the heavens and the earth."*

It is also found in Zechariah 12, talking about the endtime: *And it shall come to pass in that day, that I will seek to destroy all the nations that come against Jerusalem. And I will pour upon the house of David, and upon the inhabitants of Jerusalem, the Spirit of grace and of supplications: and they shall look upon Me **alef-tav** whom they have pierced, and they shall mourn for Him, as one mourns for his only son, and shall be in bitterness for Him, as one that is in bitterness for his firstborn.*

As the first and last letters of the Hebrew alphabet, saying alef-tav is akin to saying the Alpha and the Omega, a title Christ used to describe Himself in Revelation 1.

He is our Creator, and the volume of this book, focused on redemption, is all about Him!

John the Apostle

Saint John the Evangelist by Bernardo Cavallino (1616-1656)

Now, we believe God manifested Himself in the physical world through Jesus Christ, based largely on John's description of Jesus at the beginning of his Gospel.

"In the beginning was the Word, and the Word was with God, and the Word was God. He was in the beginning with God. All things were made through Him, and without Him, nothing was made that was made. In Him was life, and that life was the light of men. The light shines in the darkness, and the darkness has not overcome it.

The true light, which enlightens everyone, was coming into the world. He was in the world, and the world was made through Him, yet the world did not know Him. He came to His own, and His own people did not receive Him. But to all who did receive Him, to those who believed in His name, He gave the right to become children of God, who were born not of blood, nor of the will of the flesh, nor of the will of man, but of God.

And the Word became flesh and dwelt among us, and we have seen His glory, glory as of the only Son from the Father, full of grace and truth."

Paul the Apostle

Paul Writing His Epistles by Valentin de Boulogne (1620)

In Colossians Chapter 2, Paul describes Jesus as *the fullness of the Godhead dwelling bodily*. This supports the belief that every Old Testament appearance of God, including those of The Angel of the Lord (Yahweh Malak in Hebrew), was a pre-incarnate manifestation of Jesus Christ.

Naming the Animals
Genesis 2

Adam Naming the Animals by Jan Brueghel the Younger (17th century)

Then the Lord God said, "It is not good for the man to be alone; I will make a helper suitable for him." Now, out of the ground, the Lord God had formed every beast of the field and every bird of the heavens and brought them to the man to see what he would call them. Whatever the man called each living creature, that was its name. The man gave names to all the livestock, the birds of the heavens, and every beast of the field. But for Adam, no suitable helper was found.

The Lord with Adam and Eve in the Garden
Genesis 2-3

The Lord with Adam and Eve in the Garden of Eden by Jacob de Backer (1559)

So the Lord God caused a deep sleep to fall upon the man, and while he slept, He took one of his ribs and closed up the place with flesh. And the rib that the Lord God had taken from the man, He made into a woman and brought her to the man. Then the man said:

"This at last is bone of my bones and flesh of my flesh; she shall be called Woman because she was taken out of Man."

Therefore, a man shall leave his father and mother and hold fast to his wife, and they shall become one flesh. And the man and his wife were both naked and were not ashamed.

Paul tells us that in Jesus all the fullness of the Godhead dwells bodily (Colossians 2). This leads us to believe that Jesus walked with Adam and Eve (circa 4000-3070 B.C.) in the Garden.

The First Deception
Genesis 3

Adam and Eve's Original Sin by Raphaël (1519)

Now the serpent was more cunning than any other beast of the field that the Lord God had made. He said to the woman, "Did God actually say, 'You shall not eat from any tree in the garden'?" And the woman said to the serpent, "We may eat the fruit of the trees in the garden, but God said, 'You shall not eat from the fruit of the tree that is in the midst of the garden, nor shall you touch it, lest you die.'" But the serpent said to the woman, "You will not surely die. For God knows that when you eat of it, your eyes will be opened, and you will be like God, knowing good and evil." So when the woman saw that the tree was good for food, and that it was a delight to the eyes, and that the tree was desirable to make one wise, she took of its fruit and ate. She also gave some to her husband, who was with her, and he ate. Then the eyes of both were opened, and they knew they were naked. And they sewed fig leaves together and made themselves loincloths.

Seed of the Woman
Genesis 3

The Expulsion of Adam and Eve from Paradise by Benjamin West (1791)

When Adam and Eve sinned because of the serpent's deceit, God clothed them with skins. This act taught them the lesson that blood atonement is necessary for the forgiveness of sin. He promised enmity between the serpent and the woman, and between his seed and hers, then He expelled them from the garden.

God cannot tolerate sin; He demands perfection. Since we are utterly incapable of meeting this requirement, He chose to fulfill it on our behalf.

The sinless Christ was sacrificed for us. He is the prophesied seed of the woman, and the words of Genesis 3 hint at the virgin birth.

Jesus is the Word made flesh, the Bread of Life, the Light of the world, the Way and the Door, the Good Shepherd, the Resurrection and the Life, the Truth, the True Vine, the Fount of living water, the Alpha and the Omega, the Alef and the Tav. He is both the Son of Man and the Son of God, and He willingly died for you!

The Acceptable Sacrifice
Genesis 4

The Sacrifice of Abel by Arsène Robert (1870)

Cain was enraged that Abel's sacrifice of a firstling from his flock was accepted by the Lord, while his own sacrifice of the fruit from the ground he tilled was not.

And the Lord said to Cain, *"Why are you angry, and why has your face fallen? If you do well, will you not be accepted? But if you do not do well, sin is crouching at the door. Its desire is for you, but you must rule over it."*

Hebrews 11 tells us, *"By faith Abel offered to God a more acceptable sacrifice than Cain, through which he was commended as righteous, God commending him by accepting his gifts."*

Both sacrifices reflect some aspect of Christ, but God looked at the hearts of the two brothers and accepted Abel's offering because it was an offering of faith in the provision and promise of God. Cain's offering, on the other hand, was not made in faith, but in trust of his own works.

The Lord Speaks to Cain
Genesis 4

Cain and Able by Pietro Novelli (1603-1647)

But Cain did not rule over his passion. Sin prevailed, so the Lord said, *"What have you done? The voice of your brother's blood is crying to Me from the ground. And now you are cursed from the ground, which has opened its mouth to receive your brother's blood from your hand. When you work the ground, it shall no longer yield to you its strength. You shall be a fugitive and a wanderer on the earth."*

Sin crouches at the door for us as well. Its desire is for us, but we must rule over it, and we can when we walk in the Spirit.

Enoch Translated
Genesis 5

God Took Enoch by Gerard Hoet (1648-1733)

When Enoch (circa 3378-3013 B.C.) *had lived 65 years, he fathered Methuselah. Enoch walked with God for 300 years after he fathered Methuselah, and he had other sons and daughters. Thus, all the days of Enoch were 365 years, and he was not, for God took him.*

Could this be a foreshadowing of our own translation (rapture) before the tribulation?

Gospel Message
Genesis 5

Birth of Noah by James Jacques Joseph Tissot (1896-1902)

Hidden messages... When reading Scripture, reference the original language and look for patterns.

Here we have Lamech with his wife and baby Noah, but there is a message in the first ten names of Jesus' genealogical line if you look at their meanings: Adam (Man), Seth (Appointed), Enos (Mortal), Cainan (Sorrow), Mahalaleel (The Blessed God), Jared (Shall Come Down), Enoch (Teaching), Methuselah (His Death Shall Bring), Lamech (Despairing), Noah (Comfort). Here we find the Gospel message.

Man is appointed mortal, sorrow. The Blessed God shall come down, teaching that His death shall bring comfort to the despairing.

Amazing!

The Deluge
Genesis 6

Noah, The Eve of the Deluge by John Linnell (1848)

And God said to Noah (circa 2944-1994 B.C.), "I have determined to make an end of all flesh, for the earth is filled with violence because of them. Behold, I will destroy them along with the earth. Make yourself an ark of gopher wood. Make rooms in the ark and cover it inside and out with pitch. This is how you are to make it: the length of the ark shall be 300 cubits, its breadth 50 cubits, and its height 30 cubits. Make a roof for the ark and finish it to a cubit above, and set the door of the ark in its side. Make it with lower, second, and third decks. For behold, I will bring a flood of waters upon the earth to destroy all flesh that has the breath of life under heaven. Everything that is on the earth shall die."

"But I will establish My covenant with you, and you shall come into the ark—you, your sons, your wife, and your sons' wives with you. Of every living thing of all flesh, you shall bring two of every sort into the ark to keep them alive with you. They shall be male and female. Of the birds according to their kinds, and of the animals according to their kinds, of every creeping thing of the ground, according to its kind, two of every sort shall come to you to keep them alive. Also, take with you every sort of food that is eaten, and store it up. It shall serve as food for you and for them." Noah did this; he did all that God commanded him.

Clean and Unclean Animals
Genesis 7

The Animals Entering the Ark by Giovanni Francesco Castiglione (1641-1710)

Please note that God said, *"Take with you seven pairs of all clean animals, the male and his mate, and a pair of the animals that are not clean, the male and his mate, and seven pairs of the birds of the heavens also, male and female, to keep their offspring alive on the face of all the earth."*

How Noah knew which animals were clean and unclean is not explained here, but the logical assumption is that land animals that feed on plants were considered clean, while those that did not were essentially feasting on death, a result of the Fall. This assumption is supported by the types of animals deemed acceptable under the Law of Moses, which further refined the dietary laws for Israel.

Animals that chew the cud and have cloven hooves were clean. Why might this be the case? Because they reflect an aspect of faith: carefully considering and rightly dividing the Word of God, which reveals Christ.

Though Noah did not accommodate them on the ark, clean water animals must have fins and scales. Believers, like these water creatures, must be protected and properly guided by the Word of God.

Christ did away with these dietary restrictions in Mark 7.

Renewing the World
Genesis 7

Noah in the Ark by Ditlev Blunck (1835)

In the six hundredth year of Noah's life, in the second month, on the seventeenth day of the month, all the fountains of the great deep burst forth, and the windows of the heavens were opened. And rain fell upon the earth for forty days and forty nights.

The Lord Saves Noah
Genesis 7-8

Sacrifice of Noah by Pacecco de Rosa (1607-1657)

When the waters abated 150 days later, the ark came to rest on the mountains of Ararat in the seventh month, on the seventeenth day of the month. This day is now recognized as the day the Lord rose from the dead, around the same time as what would later become the Feast of Firstfruits.

Note that in these days, the calendar appears to consist of 12 months, each with 30 days. Some believe the calendar was lengthened later, during the time of Joshua.

God's Covenant with Noah
Genesis 9

Noah's Thanks Offering by Joseph Anton Koch (1803)

Then God made a covenant...

And God said, "This is the sign of the covenant that I make between Me and you and every living creature that is with you, for all future generations: I have set My bow in the cloud, and it shall be a sign of the covenant between Me and the earth. When I bring clouds over the earth and the bow is seen in the clouds, I will remember My covenant that is between Me and you and every living creature of all flesh. And the waters shall never again become a flood to destroy all flesh."

Some believe the flood was the first rainfall – *the windows of the heavens were opened*, allowing the canopy of water to fall, having been established the second day of creation.

And God said, "Let there be an expanse in the midst of the waters, and let it separate the waters from the waters." And God made the expanse and separated the waters that were below the expanse from the waters that were above the expanse. And it was so. And God called the expanse Heaven. And there was evening and there was morning, the second day. (Genesis 1)

Such a barrier would provide a higher air pressure and could account for longer life and greater size.

Tower of Babel
Genesis 11 – John 14

The Building of the Tower of Babel by Marten van Valckenborch I (1534–1612)

The whole earth had one language and the same words. And as people migrated from the east, they found a plain in the land of Shinar and settled there. They said to one another, "Come, let us make bricks and burn them thoroughly." They had brick for stone and bitumen for mortar. Then they said, "Come, let us build ourselves a city and a tower with its top in the heavens, and let us make a name for ourselves, lest we be scattered over the face of the whole earth." And the Lord came down to see the city and the tower which the children of man had built. And the Lord said, "Behold, they are one people, and they have all one language, and this is only the beginning of what they will do. Nothing they propose to do will now be impossible for them. Come, let Us go down and confuse their language, so that they may not understand one another's speech." So the Lord dispersed them from there over the face of all the earth, and they stopped building the city. Therefore, its name was called Babel, because there the Lord confused the language of all the earth.

Mankind has a need for something more, a yearning to reach God.

The Lord stopped this attempt to reach the heavens as a lesson that man cannot succeed alone. There is only one way to the heavens, Jesus Christ, who said, *"I am the way, the truth, and the life. No one comes to the Father except through Me." (John 14:6)*

The Call of Abraham
Genesis 12

Abraham's Journey from Ur to Canaan by József Molnár (1850)

The Lord said to Abram, "Go from your country, your kindred, and your father's house to the land that I will show you. I will make of you a great nation, and I will bless you and make your name great, so that you will be a blessing. I will bless those who bless you, and him who dishonors you I will curse; and in you, all the families of the earth shall be blessed."

So Abram went, as the Lord had told him, and Lot went with him. Abram was seventy-five years old when he departed from Haran. Abram took Sarai, his wife, Lot, his brother's son, and all their possessions that they had gathered, and the people they had acquired in Haran, and they set out for the land of Canaan.

The Lord begins to narrow the generational line to the Messiah—Jesus Christ, son of David, son of Judah, son of Abraham, blessing all the families of the earth.

Melchizedek
Genesis 14

The Meeting of Abraham and Melchizedek by Peter Paul Rubens (1626)

Abraham went to war against four kings to rescue his nephew, Lot, and his family, who had been taken captive from Sodom. When he succeeded, he was honored by Melchizedek, king of Salem and priest of God Most High, who offered him bread and wine.

Abraham gave him a tenth of the battle spoils, for Melchizedek was the king of righteousness, the king of peace, and a priest forever… just as Jesus Christ, the Son of God. (Hebrews 7)

God's Covenant with Abraham
Genesis 15

A Deep Sleep Fell Upon Abram is an illustration from the 1728 *Figures de la Bible*
Illustrated by Gerard Hoet (1648–1733) and others

Historians tell us those who lived at this time cut a covenant by dividing a sacrifice and walking between the pieces, indicating the same would occur to the one who failed to keep the agreement.

The Lord promised Abram that his descendants would inherit the land, but Abram asked for reassurance, so the Lord had him prepare sacrifice to make the covenant.

As the sun was going down, a deep sleep fell on Abram...When the sun had gone down and it was dark, behold, a smoking fire pot and a flaming torch passed between these pieces. On that day the Lord made a covenant with Abram, saying, "To your offspring I give this land, from the river of Egypt to the great river, the river Euphrates..."

So, the Lord made the covenant alone just as He paid the penalty for sin.

The Angel of the Lord with Hagar
Genesis 16/21

Hagar and the Angel by Giuseppe Bottani (1717 – 1784)

The Lord promised Abram heirs, but they had no children because Sarai was barren. She took it upon herself to give her handmaiden, Hagar, to Abram to conceive, which she did. But Hagar looked upon Sarai with contempt, so Sarai treated her harshly (circa 1992-1817 B.C.). Hagar fled.

The Angel of the Lord, who we believe was Jesus Christ, found her by a spring of water in the wilderness on the way to Shur, instructing her to return and submit to her mistress, adding, *"I will surely multiply your offspring so that they cannot be numbered for multitude."*

"Behold, you are pregnant and shall bear a son. You shall call his name Ishmael, because the Lord has heard your affliction. He shall be a wild donkey of a man, his hand against everyone, and everyone's hand against him. He shall dwell in opposition to all his kinsmen."

After he was weaned, Abraham reluctantly sent them away, comforted by God.

Hagar lost heart in the desert, but once again, the Angel of the Lord appeared, showed her a spring, and assured her that Ishmael would become a great nation.

The Arabs trace their heritage to Ishmael.

Abrahamic Covenant
Genesis 17

Circumcision of Jesus by Niccolò Pallavicino (1605) (originally done by Peter Paul Rubens in 1577)

The Lord changed Abram's name to Abraham and promised the land of Canaan forever to his descendants. He made a covenant...

And God said to Abraham, "As for you, you shall keep My covenant, you and your offspring after you throughout their generations. This is My covenant, which you shall keep, between Me and you and your offspring after you: Every male among you shall be circumcised. You shall be circumcised in the flesh of your foreskins, and it shall be a sign of the covenant between Me and you. He who is eight days old among you shall be circumcised. Every male throughout your generations, whether born in your house or bought with your money from any foreigner who is not of your offspring, both he who is born in your house and he who is bought with your money, shall surely be circumcised. So shall My covenant be in your flesh, an everlasting covenant."

Circumcision represents the cutting away of sin, for sin entered the world through one man. (Romans 5:12) Two thousand years later, this practice was fulfilled in Christ.

The Lord Visits Abraham
Genesis 18

Abraham Receiving the Three Angels by Bartolome Esteban Murillo (1667)

Under the oaks of Mamre, the Lord, accompanied by two angels, ate with Abraham (circa 1992-1817 B.C.), promised him a son through Sarah, who laughed, and discussed His judgment of Sodom and Gomorrah.

Lot was in Sodom, so Abraham bargained for the city, starting with fifty righteous men. The Lord patiently listened, promising that the city would survive if only ten righteous men were found.

The Lord's plan was to get Lot out.

Sodom and Gomorrah
Genesis 18-19 – Matthew 10

Sodom and Gomorrah by John Martin (1852)

We often wonder why suffering and death occur. Let us remember *the wages of sin is death, but the free gift of God is eternal life in Christ Jesus our Lord.* (Romans 6:23)

What happened to Sodom and Gomorrah, like the flood, was intended as a lesson—the consequence of living life without God. We must reflect on such events.

Lot honored God and was rescued; the rest of the city did not. Jesus Christ suffered torture and death, and His sinless, innocent sacrifice paid for the sins of the whole world… once, for all.

Jesus sent out His twelve apostles to proclaim the kingdom of God and told them, *"If anyone will not receive you or listen to your words, shake off the dust from your feet when you leave that house or town. Truly, I say to you, it will be more bearable on the day of judgment for the land of Sodom and Gomorrah than for that town."*

Learn the lesson. There is more to come. We do not have all the answers, because *now we see through a glass darkly* (1 Corinthians 13:12). Trust.

Abimelech
Genesis 20

Abraham is summoned before Abimelech; Sarah is given back to Abraham by Nicolaes Berchem (1670)

Traveling toward the Negev, Abraham feared the people might kill him to take Sarah because she was very beautiful, so he and Sarah agreed to claim they were brother and sister while traveling. In fact, she was his half-sister, daughter of his father but not his mother.

Abimelech, king of Gerar, found her desirable and took her.

But God came to Abimelech in a dream by night and said, "Behold, you are a dead man because of the woman whom you have taken, for she is a man's wife." Now, Abimelech had not approached her. So, he said, "Lord, will You kill an innocent people? Did he not himself say to me, 'She is my sister'? And she herself said, 'He is my brother.' In the integrity of my heart and the innocence of my hands I have done this." Then God said to him in the dream, "Yes, I know that you have done this in the integrity of your heart, and it was I who kept you from sinning against Me. Therefore, I did not let you touch her. Now, return the man's wife, for he is a prophet, so that he will pray for you, and you shall live. But if you do not return her, know that you shall surely die, you and all who are yours."

So, Abimelech returned Sarah and gave Abraham gifts.

Half-truths can lead to trouble, but staying true to your integrity is invaluable.

Abraham's Sacrifice
Genesis 22

The Angel of the Lord Preventing Abraham from Sacrificing his Son Isaac by Pieter Lastman (1616)

God told Abraham to take his beloved son and sacrifice him in the land of Moriah, a three-day journey.

As they climbed the mountain, Isaac asked about the sacrifice. Abraham replied that *God would provide Himself an offering.* Once there, Abraham built an altar, bound his son, and raised the knife. The Angel of the Lord stopped him and provided a ram in Isaac's place. Abraham called the place Adonai-yireh, meaning, "On the mount of the Lord, there is vision."

Indeed, God did provide Himself an offering: Jesus, the beloved Son of the Father, was sacrificed to pay for the sins of the whole world (perhaps on the very same spot), so that we could be reconciled to Him.

The Father chose to do this for us while we were yet sinners, demonstrating His unimaginable mercy.

Finding a Bride
Genesis 24

Rebecca and Eliezer by Alexandre Cabanel (1883)

Abraham sent his servant Eliezer with many gifts to Mesopotamia, to the city of Nahor, to seek a wife for Isaac. When he arrived and stood by a spring of water, he prayed:

"Let the young woman to whom I shall say, 'Please let down your jar that I may drink,' and who shall say, 'Drink, and I will water your camels'—let her be the one whom You have appointed for Your servant Isaac. By this, I shall know that You have shown steadfast love to my master."

And so it was. This beautiful young maiden, Rebekah, daughter of Bethuel, the son of Milcah, the wife of Nahor, Abraham's brother, fulfilled the prophetic prayer and agreed to accompany Eliezer to become Isaac's bride.

This story models God the Father sending His Spirit to find a bride for the Son of God.

The Effect of Beauty
Genesis 26

Plate with the coat of arms of Isabelle d'Este-Gonzague, Marchioness of Mantua, with decoration of Abimelech spying on Isaac and Rebecca by Nicholas of Urbino (1524-1525)

Isaac went to King Abimelech in Gerar because of a famine and settled there. Like his father, he feared for his life because of Rebekah's beauty, so, once again, he claimed she was his sister.

Abimelech, king of the Philistines, looked out of a window and saw Isaac laughing with Rebekah, his wife. So, Abimelech called Isaac and said, "Behold, she is your wife. How then could you say, 'She is my sister'?" Isaac said to him, "Because I thought, 'Lest I die because of her.'" Abimelech said, "What is this you have done to us? One of the people might easily have lain with your wife, and you would have brought guilt upon us." So, Abimelech warned all the people, saying, "Whoever touches this man or his wife shall surely be put to death."

I suspect Abimelech was suspicious of their claim, so he paid close attention to these new neighbors. Lies are always inadvisable.

Isaac's Blessing
Genesis 27

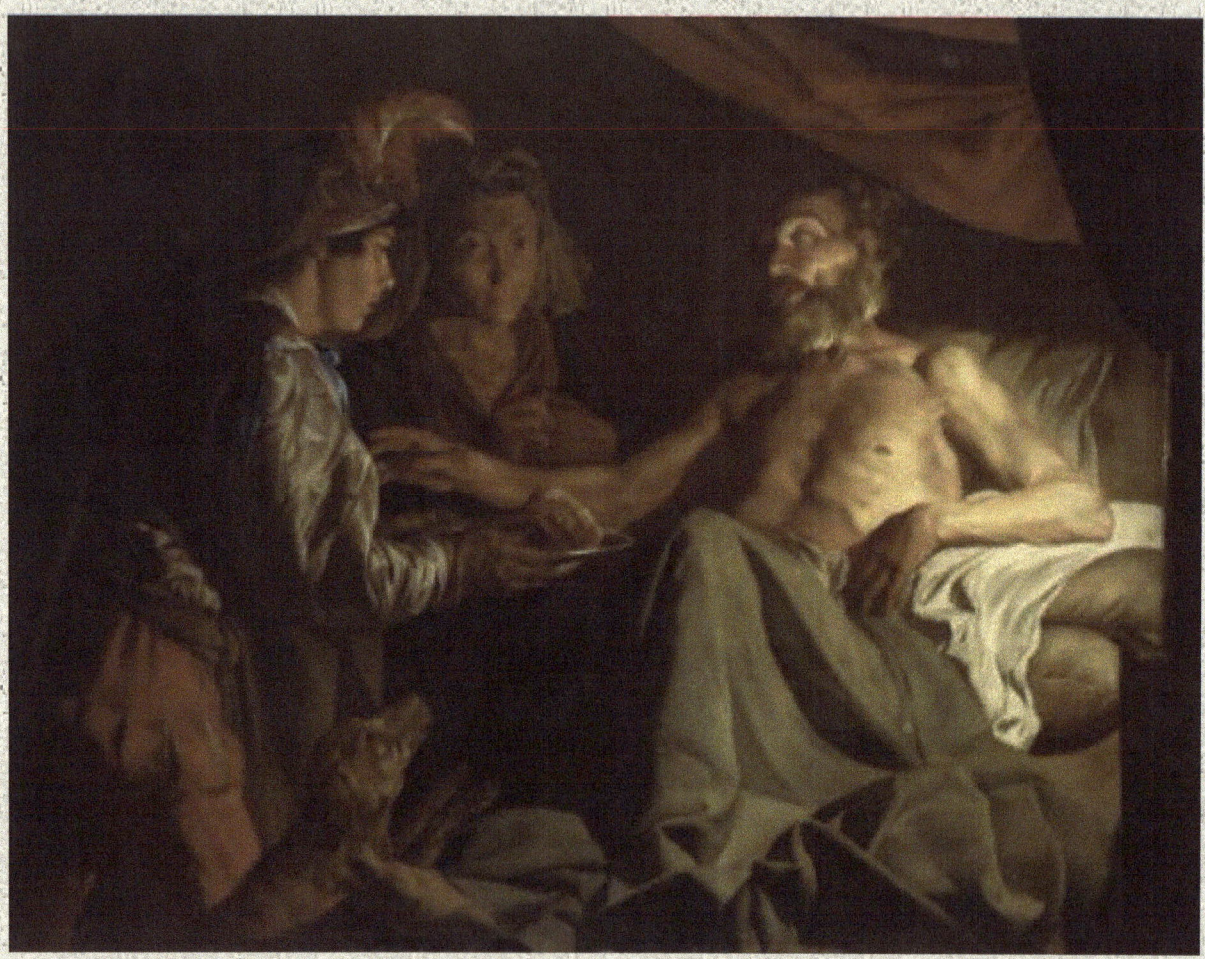

Isaac Blessing Jacob by Matthias Stom (1635)

Isaac and Rebekah had twins, Jacob and Esau, who did not get along. When they were young, Isaac favored Esau, the firstborn, and Rebekah favored Jacob, which led to division throughout much of their lives.

Jacob also took advantage of his brother. He caught Esau at a moment of weakness from hunger and bought his birthright for a bowl of stew. Later, with his mother's help, he lied to his father when he was old and blind, claiming to be Esau in order to gain his father's blessing.

Esau was outraged and swore to kill Jacob.

Bridge between Heaven and Earth
Genesis 28

Jacob's Dream by Luther Terry (1852)

And so, Jacob fled to his Uncle Laban's in Paddan-aram. On the journey…

He came to a certain place and stayed there that night because the sun had set. Taking one of the stones of the place, he put it under his head and lay down to sleep. And he dreamed, and behold, there was a ladder set up on the earth, and the top of it reached to heaven. And behold, the angels of God were ascending and descending on it! And behold, the Lord stood above it and said, "I am the Lord, the God of Abraham your father and the God of Isaac. The land on which you lie I will give to you and your offspring. Your offspring shall be like the dust of the earth, and you shall spread abroad to the west, the east, the north, and the south. And in you and your offspring shall all the families of the earth be blessed. Behold, I am with you and will keep you wherever you go, and I will bring you back to this land. For I will not leave you until I have done what I have promised you." Then Jacob awoke from his sleep and said, "Surely the Lord is in this place, and I did not know it." And he was afraid and said, "How awesome is this place! This is none other than the house of God, and this is the gate of heaven."

He saw the bridge to heaven in his dream, which is Christ in reality—who opened the way for man's reconciliation with God.

Good from Evil
Genesis 28 – 31

Jacob's Departure from Laban by Luca Giordano (1705)

When Jacob arrived at Laban's home, he fell in love with Laban's daughter, Rachel, and agreed to work tending the sheep and goats for seven years to win her hand in marriage. But on the wedding day, Laban substituted Rachel's older sister, Leah, explaining that the older must marry first. Jacob worked another seven years for both.

The sisters competed for Jacob's love by having children. Leah bore him his first four sons: Reuben, Simeon, Levi, and Judah. When Rachel saw that she was barren, she gave Jacob her handmaiden, Bilhah, to become a surrogate mother on her behalf. Bilhah then gave birth to Dan and Naphtali. Leah, no longer having children of her own, decided to do the same with her maidservant, Zilpah, who bore Gad and Asher. Leah then became pregnant again and had three more children: Issachar, Zebulun, and their only daughter, Dinah. Finally, God opened Rachel's womb, and she gave birth to Joseph, who became Jacob's favorite son. Jacob thought it was time to leave Laban.

But Laban had other plans. He had become wealthy due to Jacob's work, so he wanted Jacob to stay. Laban proposed that livestock of a particular color would become Jacob's, but he attempted to sabotage the deal to remain wealthier. Jacob stayed, and his flocks outgrew Laban's. Eventually, Jacob left to return to his homeland.

Others planned evil for Jacob, but good prevailed. Others planned evil for Christ, but good resulted.

The Lord with Jacob
Genesis 32

Jacob Wrestling with the Angel by Alexander Louis Leloir (1865)

The day before Jacob (circa 1832-1685 B.C.) met his brother Esau, he wrestled with a man who refused to give His name. The man gave Jacob the name Israel and blessed him. Jacob then called the place Peniel, which means "the face of God."

Reconciliation
Genesis 33

Meeting Between Esau and Jacob by Giovanni Maria Bottala (1636-1641)

Jacob's return meant he would have to face his past. Esau had sworn to kill Jacob because of his deceit, so Jacob had to plan carefully.

He prepared by sending gifts, servants, and parts of his large family ahead in small groups to soften his brother's heart.

Esau arrived with an army to greet Jacob, not in hatred, as was feared, but as long-lost brothers, with love and tears.

This change in Esau's heart is remarkable, as this meeting reminds us of our reconciliation to God the Father through Jesus Christ.

Rape of Dinah
Genesis 34

Rape of Dinah by Guiliano Bugiardini (15th-16th century)

Jacob settled in Canaan. His daughter, Dinah, went to visit the women of the land in the city of Shechem.

Hamor the Hivite was the prince of the land. When his son, Shechem, saw Dinah, he seized and raped her, then asked his father to obtain her for marriage.

Hamor attempted to negotiate, but Dinah's brothers deceitfully said they would not consent unless the men of the city were circumcised. The men of the city agreed, and they underwent circumcision.

On the third day after the circumcision, the men of the city were in great pain. Then Dinah's brothers, Simeon and Levi, took their swords, slew every male in the city, and plundered everything of value.

Revenge seems only fair, but evil thrives in the absence of the divine. *Vengeance is Mine, I will repay, says the Lord.* (Romans 12:19)

Death of Rachel
Genesis 35

The Death of Rachel by Gustav Metz (1847)

Jacob's family was traveling from Bethel to Bethlehem when Rachel died giving birth to her second son, Benjamin. Her tomb can still be found on that road today.

The most amazing and wonderful act of any woman is giving life to a child. Rest in peace.

Dreams
Genesis 37

Joseph Reveals His Dream to His Brethren by James Jacques Joseph Tissot (1896-1902)

Now Israel loved Joseph more than any of his other sons, because he was the son of his old age. And he made him a robe of many colors. When his brothers saw that their father loved him more than all of them, they hated him and could not speak peacefully to him.

Joseph had a dream, and when he told it to his brothers, they hated him even more. He said to them, "Hear this dream that I have dreamed: Behold, we were binding sheaves in the field, and my sheaf arose and stood upright. And your sheaves gathered around it and bowed down to my sheaf." His brothers said to him, "Are you indeed to reign over us? Or are you indeed to rule over us?" So they hated him even more for his dreams and for his words.

Then he dreamed another dream and told it to his brothers, saying, "Behold, I have dreamed another dream: The sun, the moon, and eleven stars were bowing down to me." But when he told it to his father and to his brothers, his father rebuked him and said, "What is this dream that you have dreamed? Shall I and your mother and your brothers indeed come to bow ourselves to the ground before you?" And his brothers were jealous of him, but his father kept the saying in mind.

Rejected by His Brothers
Genesis 37

Joseph Sold by His Brothers by Giovanni Maria Bottala (1636-1642)

Now his brothers went to pasture their father's flock near Shechem. And Israel said to Joseph, "Are not your brothers pasturing the flock at Shechem? Come, I will send you to them." And he said to him, "Here I am." So, he said to him, "Go now, see if it is well with your brothers and with the flock, and bring me word." So, he sent him from the Valley of Hebron, and he came to Shechem. And a man found him wandering in the fields. And the man asked him, "What are you seeking?" "I am seeking my brothers," he said. "Tell me, please, where they are pasturing the flock." And the man said, "They have gone away, for I heard them say, 'Let us go to Dothan.'" So, Joseph went after his brothers and found them at Dothan.

They saw him coming and decided to do away with him because of their hatred, so they sold him into slavery to Midianites, foreshadowing Christ's rejection by the Israelites.

Jacob Mourns His Son
Genesis 37

Jacob Mourns His Son Joseph by James Jacques Joseph Tissot (1896-1902)

Then they took Joseph's robe and slaughtered a goat and dipped the robe in the blood. And they sent the robe of many colors and brought it to their father and said, "This we have found; please identify whether it is your son's robe or not." And he identified it and said, "It is my son's robe. A fierce animal has devoured him. Joseph is without doubt torn to pieces." Then Jacob tore his garments and put sackcloth on his loins and mourned for his son many days. All his sons and all his daughters rose up to comfort him, but he refused to be comforted and said, "No, I shall go down to Sheol to my son, mourning." Thus, his father wept for him. Meanwhile the Midianites had sold him in Egypt to Potiphar, an officer of Pharaoh, the captain of the guard.

Judah and Tamar
Genesis 38

Judah and Tamar by Ferdinand Bol (1644)

Judah, son of Jacob, married the first of his three sons, Er, to Tamar, but Er died before they had children. Judah then had his second, Onan, take the role of kinsman-redeemer, but he too died before they had children.

Time passed and Judah didn't give Tamar to his third son, Shelah, so Tamar veiled herself and played the role of a harlot with Judah while he was visiting his livestock. She requested Judah's signet, cord, and staff until he paid her the young goat he promised for her services, but she was gone when he tried to pay.

About three months later Judah was told, "Tamar your daughter-in-law has been immoral. Moreover, she is pregnant by immorality." And Judah said, "Bring her out, and let her be burned." As she was being brought out, she sent word to her father-in-law, "By the man to whom these belong, I am pregnant." And she said, "Please identify whose these are, the signet and the cord and the staff." Then Judah identified them and said, "She is more righteous than I, since I did not give her to my son Shelah." And he did not know her again.

Their son, **Perez**, is Christ's ancestor. God works through imperfect people.

Potiphar's Wife
Genesis 39

Joseph and Potiphar's Wife by Guido Reni (1630)

Joseph was an outstanding steward of Potiphar's household, but his wife took too much interest in him, and after many refusals, she seized his cloak and accused him of attempted rape.

Potiphar threw him in prison.

Interpreting Dreams
Genesis 40

Joseph Interprets the Dreams While in Prison by James Jacques Joseph Tissot (1896-1902)

In prison, he met Pharoah's baker and cupbearer, who had angered the king.

One night they both had dreams which only Joseph understood and explained. In three days, the baker would be put to death and the cupbearer would return to serve Pharoah, and so it came to be, just as predicted.

Analogous to what happened at the cross, where one of the two thieves was saved.

Pharaoh's Signet Ring
Genesis 41

Joseph Receiving Pharaoh's Ring by Giovanni Battista Tiepolo (1733-1735)

When Pharoah had a dream that required interpretation, the cupbearer recalled Joseph, who was summoned by the king.

The dream predicted seven years of plenty followed by seven years of drought, and he advised Pharaoh to appoint a wise man to save Egypt through this time.

Pharaoh thought there was no one better than the one who had the wisdom of God Almighty, thus he gave his symbol of power to Joseph.

Joseph did not rely on his own skill, but listened to God, who had been speaking to him from a young age.

Joseph
Genesis 37-50

Joseph Recognized by His Brothers by Jean-Charles Tardieu (1788)

Joseph's story takes up a huge portion of Genesis. He saved Egypt (Gentile) and his own family (Israel). First born of his mother, Rachel, he was a shepherd who was most favored by his father, Jacob, but hated by his brethren. Betrayed and falsely accused of wrongdoing, he spent time with two others, one of whom was saved. He was exulted by Pharaoh, ruled to save all, and married a gentile bride. He revealed himself to his brothers in a time of trouble, and they accepted his headship. He brought his family into the land where they were honored by Pharaoh because of their relationship to him.

Curiously, this models the life of Jesus, the only begotten Son of God.

Double Portion
Genesis 48

Jacob Blessing Ephraim and Manasseh, by Benjamin West (1766-1768)

Joseph brought his family to Egypt, including Jacob. Pharaoh welcomed them warmly giving them the best of the land.

Joseph had married an Egyptian and had two boys, Manasseh and Ephraim. Jacob blessed them putting his right hand on the younger because he would become greater.

And he blessed Joseph and said, "The God before whom my fathers Abraham and Isaac walked, the God who has been my Shepherd all my life long to this day, the angel who has redeemed me from all evil, bless the boys; and in them let my name be carried on, and the name of my fathers Abraham and Isaac; and let them grow into a multitude in the midst of the earth."

Thus, Ephraim and Manasseh joined Joseph's brothers as heirs, Joseph receiving a double portion as Rachel's firstborn.

Jacob blesses His Sons
Genesis 49

The Death of Jacob by Pietro Benvenuti (1769-1844)

Jacob gave a prophetic blessing to each of his sons on his deathbed.

To Judah he said ...*your brothers will praise you; your hand will be on the neck of your enemies; your father's sons will bow down to you. You are a lion's cub, O Judah; you return from the prey, my son. Like a lion he crouches and lies down, like a lioness--who dares to rouse him? The scepter will not depart from Judah, nor the ruler's staff from between his feet, until He comes to whom it belongs and the obedience of the nations is His. He will tether his donkey to a vine, His colt to the choicest branch; He will wash his garments in wine, His robes in the blood of grapes. His eyes will be darker than wine, His teeth whiter than milk.*

In Revelation 5, John is told *Do not weep. See, the Lion of the tribe of Judah, the Root of David, has conquered, so that He can open the scroll and its seven seals.*

Jesus is Judah's descendent. He is the Lamb and the Lion. He rode into Jerusalem on a colt, and His robes were, and will be, soaked in blood. He bears the scepter to rule, and the nations will be His.

The Suffering of Job
Job

Job and His Friends by Ilya Repin (1869)

When the Lord asked Satan to consider Job as a model believer, Satan argued Job only served because he was blessed and covered by a protective hedge. To prove His point, the Lord removed Job's protections, allowing Satan to harass him as long as he did not take Job's life.

Job lost nearly everything; his children, his livestock, and his health. His wife told him to *curse God and die*, but Job replied... *You speak as one of the foolish women speaks. Shall we indeed accept good from God, and shall we not accept adversity?* (Job 2)

His friends came to comfort him, but ended up accusing him of some guilt, despite Job's insistence he was innocent of any wrongdoing. Job did not understand his circumstance but refused to blame God, saying...

Though He slay me, yet will I trust in Him... (Job 13) and claiming ... *I know that my Redeemer lives, and at the last He will stand upon the earth. And after my skin has been thus destroyed, yet in my flesh I shall see God...* (Job 19)

The Redeemer is Jesus Christ, who, like Job, did not want to suffer, but did so without accusing the Father, knowing there was purpose in our circumstance, and trusting His plan. In the end, Job was restored and Christ resurrected.

Saved from the Waters
Exodus 1-2

Moses Saved from the River by Nicolas Poussin (1638)

The time came when a Pharoah did not know of Joseph, and he believed there were too many Hebrews in Egypt, so he enslaved them, but their numbers kept growing. He then told the midwives to kill all males at birth, but they did not, fearing God, and telling Pharoah the males are born before they arrive, so eventually Pharoah told the people to toss all males in the Nile River.

Now a man from the house of Levi went and took as his wife a Levite woman. The woman conceived and bore a son, and when she saw that he was a fine child, she hid him three months. When she could hide him no longer, she took for him a basket made of bulrushes and daubed it with bitumen and pitch. She put the child in it and placed it among the reeds by the river bank. And his sister stood at a distance to know what would be done to him. Now the daughter of Pharaoh... saw the basket among the reeds and sent her servant woman, and she took it. When she opened it, she saw the child, and behold, the baby was crying. She took pity on him and said, "This is one of the Hebrews' children." Then his sister said to Pharaoh's daughter, "Shall I go and call you a nurse from the Hebrew women to nurse the child for you?" And Pharaoh's daughter said to her, "Go." So, the girl went and called the child's mother. And Pharaoh's daughter said to her, "Take this child away and nurse him for me, and I will give you your wages." So, the woman took the child and nursed him. When the child grew older, she brought him to Pharaoh's daughter, and he became her son. She named him Moses, "Because," she said, "I drew him out of the water."

Feeding the Sheep
Exodus 2

Moses and the Daughters of Jethro by Ciro Ferri (1633-1689)

Moses was a Hebrew child raised as royalty by Pharaoh's daughter. He fled Egypt for Midian when Pharaoh demanded his death for defending his countrymen and killing an Egyptian.

While resting at a well, Jethro's seven daughters came to feed their flock, but after they had drawn water, more shepherds arrived and drove them off to feed their own flock. Moses, a trained warrior, defended the daughters and forced the shepherds to leave. He finished by graciously watering their sheep.

Moses modeled Christ, leaving his royalty aside, becoming a servant, defending the powerless, and feeding the sheep.

I AM
Exodus 3 – John 8

Burning Bush by Sébastien Bourdon (17th century)

While Moses (circa 1393-1273 B.C.) was tending the flock, God called him to free His people, Israel, from Egyptian bondage. God spoke to him through a burning bush. Moses asked who should he say sent him. God responded *"I AM who I AM. Tell them I AM sent you."*

When queried by the Pharisees about Abraham, Jesus replied, *"Before Abraham was, I AM,"* so we believe Jesus Christ was the voice of the burning bush.

Ten Plagues on Egypt
Exodus 7-12

The Plague of Flies by James Jacques Joseph Tissot (1896-1902)

There came a time during Israel's sojourn in Egypt when a pharaoh forgot how Joseph saved the nation. Egypt enslaved the Israelites until God called Moses to free them.

God brought ten plagues on the Egyptians to persuade Pharaoh to let the Israelites go; they were designed to challenge the gods they worshipped: 1st turned the Nile into blood (Khnum, Hapi, and Osiris), 2nd frogs (Hapi and Heket), 3rd gnats (Seb), 4th flies (Uatchit), 5th livestock die (Ptah, Mnevis, Hathor, and Amon), 6th boils (Sekhmet, Serapis, and Imhotep), 7th hail (Nut, Isis, Seth, and Shu), 8th locusts (Serapia), 9th darkness (Re, Amon-re, Aten, Atum, Horus, and Thoth), and 10th death of the firstborn (All including Pharoah).

The Egyptian gods were impotent.

Passover
Exodus 12

And There Was a Great Cry in Egypt by Arthur Hacker (1897)

The last was the killing of the firstborn. God instructed the Israelites to kill a male lamb without blemish and spread his blood on the doorposts of their homes.

On the night of the 14th of Nisan, God went through the land and killed the firstborn of every living thing, man and beast, unless He observed the blood on the doorposts.

In the middle of the night, Pharaoh called Moses and released the people.

The Pain of Loss
Exodus 12

Lamentations over the Death of the First-Born of Egypt by Charles Sprague Pearce (1877)

There is no way to measure the depth of the pain of the loss of one's firstborn, especially on such a scale. It is devastating. It is debilitating. On humans.

How do you imagine the Lord responds?

Jesus, His only Begotten Son, is our Passover. His death, on the 14th of Nisan, paid the debt of the whole world. We are reconciled to God with the covering of His blood.

You need only accept the gift.

Pillar of Light
Exodus 13

The Israelites Crossing the Desert by William West (1845)

When Pharaoh let the people go, God did not lead them by way of the land of the Philistines, although that was nearby. For God said, "Lest the people change their minds when they see war and return to Egypt." But God led the people around by the way of the wilderness toward the Red Sea. And the people of Israel went up out of the land of Egypt equipped for battle. Moses took the bones of Joseph with him, for Joseph had made the sons of Israel solemnly swear, saying, "God will surely visit you, and you shall carry up my bones with you from here." And they moved on from Succoth and encamped at Etham, on the edge of the wilderness. And the Lord went before them by day in a pillar of cloud to lead them along the way, and by night in a pillar of fire to give them light, that they might travel by day and by night. The pillar of cloud by day and the pillar of fire by night did not depart from before the people.

Crossing the Red Sea
Exodus 14

Crossing the Red Sea by Luca Giordano (1681)

And the Israelites crossed the Red Sea, where the Lord engulfed the pursuing Egyptian forces.

The People were Protected
Exodus 15

Song of Miriam the Prophetess by Luca Giordano (1687)

The Israelites left Egypt, crossing the Sinai and the Red Sea always being pursued by Pharoah and his army, but the Lord was continually protecting His chosen, and after the Red Sea crossing, Miriam celebrated.

Then Miriam the prophetess, the sister of Aaron, took a tambourine in her hand, and all the women went out after her with tambourines and dancing. And Miriam sang to them:

"Sing to the Lord, for He has triumphed gloriously; the horse and his rider He has thrown into the sea."

Manna
Exodus 16

The Israelites Gathering the Manna in the Desert by Nicolas Poussin (1637-1639)

A month after the Exodus, the people complained about what they would eat in the wilderness. God gave them the bread of angels, which the people called "manna," meaning "What is it?" It had the appearance of coriander seed and the taste of honey wafers. Each person had to gather their own, but it would spoil if kept overnight, except on the sixth day, when they were to gather twice as much, so they could rest on the seventh day to remember creation. The bread ended when they crossed the Jordan and entered the promised land, some forty years later.

Jesus Christ is the bread of life who came from heaven. He is the Word made flesh. He tells us if we eat his flesh (bread) and drink His blood (wine), we will live forever. Our lives ought to be sustained by the Word, to take in, and live by it daily so we would grow into His image.

The Blessing
Numbers 6

Moses and Aaron Speak to the People by James Jacques Joseph Tissot (1896-1902)

The Lord spoke to Moses, saying, "Speak to Aaron and his sons, saying, Thus you shall bless the people of Israel: you shall say to them,

> *The Lord bless you and keep you;*
> *the Lord make his face to shine upon you and be gracious to you;*
> *the Lord lift up his countenance upon you and give you peace.*

"So shall they put My name upon the people of Israel, and I will bless them."

Stay in touch. Pray. Paul said, *Rejoice always, pray without ceasing, give thanks in all circumstances; for this is the will of God in Christ Jesus for you.* (1 Thessalonians 5)

Land of Milk and Honey
Numbers 13-14

The Grapes of Canaan by James Jacques Joseph Tissot (1896-1902)

The Lord spoke to Moses, saying, "Send men to spy out the land of Canaan, which I am giving to the people of Israel..."

So, they went up and spied out the land from the wilderness of Zin to Rehob, near Lebo-hamath. They went up into the Negeb and came to Hebron. Ahiman, Sheshai, and Talmai, the descendants of Anak, were there. (Hebron was built seven years before Zoan in Egypt.) And they came to the Valley of Eshcol and cut down from there a branch with a single cluster of grapes, and they carried it on a pole between two of them; they also brought some pomegranates and figs.

When the twelve spies returned, only Joshua and Caleb encouraged the people to take this marvelous land of milk and honey. The rest fearfully reported there were giants in the land and the people refused to go, so God made them wander for forty years.

Moses and the Rock
Exodus 17 - Numbers 20

Moses Striking the Rock by Nicolas Poussin (1649)

During their wilderness wanderings, there was little water. Twice God provided water from rocks. The first time, He told Moses to strike the rock and water would flow. The second time He told Moses to speak to the rock, but in frustration, Moses struck the rock and water flowed. God reprimanded Moses for not following His direction and punished him by not letting him enter the Promised Land.

Jesus is the Rock. The first time He came, He was smitten. The second time He comes, He will conquer and rule.

The Fight with Amalek
Exodus 17

Praying Moses with Aaron and Hur on Mount Horeb by Joseph von Führich (1832)

Israel encamped at Rephidim, and the people complained for lack of water. The Lord instructed Moses to strike the rock at Horeb which brought forth water.

Now Amalek came and fought with Israel. Joshua led the battle against him, while Moses observed from the hill.

As long as Moses held his hands high, Israel prevailed, but when he tired and his hands fell, Amalek prevailed. So, Aaron, the high priest, and Hur, whose name means light, sat Moses on a rock, supporting his hands until sunset, and Joshua overwhelmed the people of Amalek with the sword.

The story can be viewed as an allegory of the struggle between the spirit and the flesh. Christ, the smittened rock, provides the water of the Spirit. The flesh (Amalek) wars against the spirit, which prevails as long as God is preeminent, requiring the support of prayer (high priest) and the Word (light). Joshua is a form of the Hebrew name for Jesus, bearing the sword, which is the Word of God.

Jesus is the Word made flesh, the fount of living water, the light of the world, and every story points to Him!

Receiving the Law
Exodus 31

Moses Receives the Tablets of the Law by João Zeferino da Costa (1868)

The Lord came down on Mount Sinai (Exodus 19-20) in thunder, lightning, smoke, and the sound of trumpets and spoke the Ten Commandments directly to the Israelites who were afraid and asked Moses to be their intercessor with God. Then Moses was called to the summit to learn more for forty days and nights (time of testing).

The Lord gave Moses the Law in person on the holy mountain during the Exodus. In time, this expands to what is now considered the 613 commandments contained in the Law of Moses. Many try to keep this law, which serves as the foundation of both a moral code and legal obligations accepted today around the world.

If our original parents could not keep one commandment, what makes us think we could keep ten or 613? Why was the law even given?

Paul tells us the law was given to increase the trespass (Romans 5:20). While the law is perfect, we are not, nor can we ever live up to the standard on our own. Belief in Jesus Christ makes the way.

Outrage
Exodus 32 - Deuteronomy 9

Moses and the Golden Calf by Domenico Gargiulo (1609-1675)

The Israelites convinced Aaron to make an idol of a golden calf while Moses was on the mountain. How quickly we turn to something we can see and touch.

Moses was so outraged when he returned, he threw the stone tablets, and punished the people for their idolatry.

Moses spent another forty days on the mountaintop pleading for God's mercy for the Israelites and obtaining new tablets.

Mankind will never learn while they rely on law, which is why the Lord's solution was to pay the penalty Himself, and work with individuals from within. Thank you, Father, for the gift of Jesus Christ and the Holy Spirit.

Tabernacle
Exodus 40

The Israelites' Encampment in the Wilderness, Guided by God by J. J. Derghi (1866)

The Tabernacle was isolated by a white linen fence, resting on bronze sockets (symbol of suffering), with a single entrance. Inside the fence before the Tabernacle was the altar of sacrifice and the laver of washing. The Tabernacle rested on silver sockets (symbol of blood), and inside was the light of the menorah, the table of showbread, and the altar of incense, which stood at the veil separating the Holy Place from the Holy of Holies, where the Ark of the Covenant rested, containing the stone tablets, the Ten Commandments, the Word of God.

Jesus Christ is the way, the truth, and the life. No one comes to the Father except through Him. He was sacrificed for us, and we wash in His Word. He is the light of the world and the bread of life. The veil was torn, top to bottom upon His death, and He lives to make intercession (altar of incense) for us. He is the Word made flesh.

Ark of the Covenant
Exodus 40

Moses and Joshua Before the Tabernacle by James Jacques Joseph Tissot (1896-1902)

Leaders facing the Ark of the Covenant placed inside the Tabernacle's Holy of Holies. It eventually contained the tablets of stone, a golden pot of manna, and Aaron's staff that budded. (Hebrews 9)

Note: This work is misnamed. The man on the right is wearing the High Priest's breastplate. Neither Moses nor Joshua were High Priests. Aaron was the first High Priest, followed by his son, Eleazar.

Brass Serpent
Numbers 21

Moses and the Brazen Serpent by Peter Paul Rubens (1610)

During the wilderness wanderings, God punished the Israelites with fiery serpents because they continually complained, not trusting Him. Many died. When Moses petitioned God to relent, He was instructed to mount a brass serpent on a pole, and those who looked upon the serpent (sin crucified) would be saved.

Jesus Christ was made sin for us and crucified upon a pole. Those who gaze upon Him will be saved.

And why did He do it?

That in the ages to come He might show the exceeding riches of His grace in His kindness toward us through Christ Jesus. (Ephesians 2:7)

The Angel of the Lord with Balaam and his Donkey
Numbers 22-24

Landscape with Balaam by Joseph Anton Koch (1832-1836)

Balak, leader of the Moabites, asked Balaam to curse Israel as they crossed the land. The Lord told Balaam not to do it, so he declined the offer.

The Moabites came again. This time the Lord told Balaam to go but to follow His directions. Balaam saddled his donkey and left the following morning. This angered the Lord, so the Angel of the Lord drew His sword and took a stand to block his way.

Three times the donkey saw the Angel of the Lord and turned aside. Each time Balaam became angry and struck the donkey with his staff.

The Lord opened the donkey's mouth, who asked why he was being punished, because his turning aside was not his normal routine. Balaam threatened to kill the donkey, and then became aware of the Angel of the Lord, who told him He would have killed Balaam had the donkey not turned aside.

Balaam bowed down and fell on his face, apologizing for his actions. The Angel of the Lord let Balaam continue his journey to Balak, with the insistence he follow orders.

In the end, Balaam spent time with Balak but blessed Israel rather than curse in accordance with the Lord's wishes.

Seduction
Numbers 25

Phinehas Slaying Zimri and Kozbi the Midianite by Jeremias van Winghe (1585-1645)

But Balaam was not done. He could not curse Israel but advised they were vulnerable to seduction, so the women of the land made themselves available and enticed the Israelites to worship their false god, Baal of Peor, which angered the Lord (Revelation 2:14). There was a call for death.

Zimri, leader of a father's house, brought Cozbi (the name means Lying), a leader's daughter, to the camp for intercourse. Phinehas, Aaron's grandson, saw this leader's actions, took a javelin, and killed the pair in the act, which stopped the killing, having claimed 24,000 lives.

And the Lord said to Moses, "Phinehas the son of Eleazar, son of Aaron the priest, has turned back My wrath from the people of Israel, in that he was jealous with My jealousy among them, so that I did not consume the people of Israel in My jealousy. Therefore, say, 'Behold, I give to him My Covenant of peace, and it shall be to him and to his descendants after him the covenant of a perpetual priesthood, because he was jealous for his God and made atonement for the people of Israel.'"

Phinehas, now a priest forever, is like Christ.

Unauthorized Fire
Leviticus 10

The Dead Bodies Carried Away by James Jacques Joseph Tissot (1896-1902)

Now Nadab and Abihu, the sons of Aaron, each took his censer and put fire in it and laid incense on it and offered unauthorized fire before the Lord, which He had not commanded them. And fire came out from before the Lord and consumed them, and they died before the Lord. Then Moses said to Aaron, "This is what the Lord has said: 'Among those who are near Me I will be sanctified, and before all the people I will be glorified.'" And Aaron held his peace.

And Moses called Mishael and Elzaphan, the sons of Uzziel, the uncle of Aaron, and said to them, "Come near; carry your brothers away from the front of the sanctuary and out of the camp." So, they came near and carried them in their coats out of the camp, as Moses had said. And Moses said to Aaron and to Eleazar and Ithamar his sons, "Do not let the hair of your heads hang loose, and do not tear your clothes, lest you die, and wrath come upon all the congregation; but let your brothers, the whole house of Israel, bewail the burning that the Lord has kindled. And do not go outside the entrance of the tent of meeting, lest you die, for the anointing oil of the Lord is upon you." And they did according to the word of Moses.

Daughters of Zelophehad
Numbers 27

The Daughters of Zelophehad, Illustration from The Bible and Its Story Taught by One Thousand Picture Lessons. Edited by Charles F. Horne and Julius A. Bewer (1908)

Zelophehad's daughters complained to Moses they ought to receive an inheritance since their father had no sons. Moses turned to Yahweh who agreed daughters with no brothers may inherit if they marry within the tribe.

Mary had no brothers and married Joseph, who was also of the tribe of Judah. She inherited from her father, whose ancestry was David's son Nathan.

Joseph descended from Jeconiah, last of David's line serving on the throne, who was so evil that Yahweh declared a blood curse (Jeremiah 22) on his descendants, stating none would ever hold the throne.

Jesus' legal claim on the throne hinges on the virgin birth, predicted by Isaiah 7:14 and the inheritance procedures as modified in the request made by Zelophehad's daughters.

Cities of Refuge
Numbers 35

The City of Refuge by George Tinworth for Doulton & Co (2007)

Rather than prisons or police in ancient Israel, murder was avenged by the next of kin, called the Avenger of Blood. If a death was accidental, the accused could seek refuge in one of six cities. They were freed completely upon the death of the high priest.

On the cross, Jesus Christ asked the Father to forgive them for they did not know what they were doing. He is our City of Refuge, we are secure in Him, and as our high priest, we were freed upon His death.

Cleansing a House
Leviticus 14

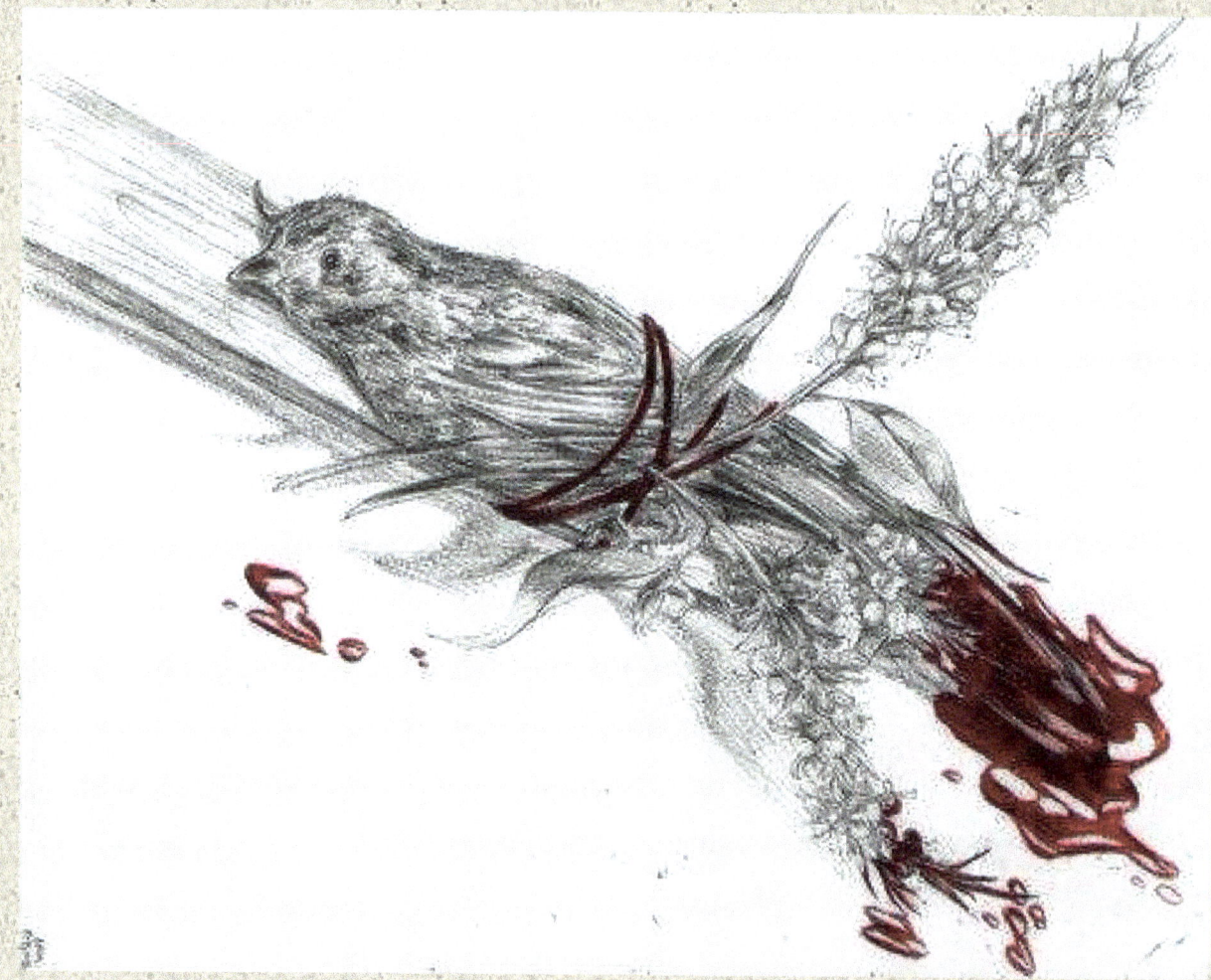

Aspergillum as Described in Leviticus by Julia O'Gara (2011)

There were specific cleansing rituals in ancient Israel…

And for the cleansing of the house, he shall take two small birds, with cedarwood and scarlet yarn and hyssop, and shall kill one of the birds in an earthenware vessel over fresh water and shall take the cedarwood and the hyssop and the scarlet yarn, along with the live bird, and dip them in the blood of the bird that was killed and in the fresh water and sprinkle the house seven times. Thus, he shall cleanse the house with the blood of the bird and with the fresh water and with the live bird and with the cedarwood and hyssop and scarlet yarn. And he shall let the live bird go out of the city into the open country. So, he shall make atonement for the house, and it shall be clean.

The soldiers used hyssop to feed wine vinegar to Christ hanging on a cedarwood cross. His blood frees us, and the scarlet yarn reminds us of this sacrificial atonement.

Levitical Sacrifices
Leviticus 23

Sacrifice of Moses by Massimo Stanzione (1650)

God ordained continual, abundant, and bloody sacrifice of innocent animals to atone for the sins of the Israelites, which included the burnt offering, meal offering, peace offering, sin offering, and trespass offering.

Substitution
Leviticus 23

The Scapegoat by William Holman Hunt (1854-1855)

The Levitical system also included specific feasts, including the Day of Atonement, which used a scapegoat. Two goats were chosen, and by lot, one was released to disappear in the wilderness while the blood of the other covered sin.

Jesus Christ was sacrificed once for all to reconcile us to the Father. Each sacrifice/feast represents some aspect of Christ's mission as our intercessor with God.

Death of Moses
Deuteronomy 34

The Death of Moses by Musée Fabre (1850)

Then Moses went up from the plains of Moab to Mount Nebo, to the top of Pisgah, which is opposite Jericho. And the Lord showed him all the land, Gilead as far as Dan, all Naphtali, the land of Ephraim and Manasseh, all the land of Judah as far as the western sea, the Negeb, and the Plain, that is, the Valley of Jericho the city of palm trees, as far as Zoar. And the Lord said to him, "This is the land of which I swore to Abraham, to Isaac, and to Jacob, 'I will give it to your offspring.' I have let you see it with your eyes, but you shall not go over there." So, Moses the servant of the Lord died there in the land of Moab, according to the word of the Lord, and He buried him in the valley in the land of Moab opposite Beth-peor; but no one knows the place of his burial to this day. Moses was 120 years old when he died. His eye was undimmed, and his vigor unabated. And the people of Israel wept for Moses in the plains of Moab thirty days. Then the days of weeping and mourning for Moses were ended.

Rahab
Joshua 2

Rahab and the Emissaries of Joshua (17th century, artist unknown)

After the death of Moses, Joshua led the Israelites to take possession of the land promised to Abraham. Jericho was their first major battle on the west side of the Jordan.

Joshua sent two men into Jericho to spy out the walled city, and they lodged in the house of Rahab. Soldiers of the city came to take the strangers, but Rahab hid them and misled the soldiers on their whereabouts.

Rahab helped the men escape, letting them through a window, down the wall and advised them to hide in the mountains for three days. She told them she knew that God had given them the land, and they promised to save those in her house, telling her to mark her house on the wall with a scarlet cord.

Rahab is an ancestor of Jesus. Her son is Boaz. The scarlet cord protects her family like the blood on the doorpost in the Passover. The three days remind us of Jesus' time in the grave.

The Lord with Joshua
Joshua 5

The Captain of the Lord's Army Appears to Joshua by Ferdinand Bol (1616-1680)

The Commander of the Lord's army met Joshua (circa 1355-1245 B.C.) on the eve of the attack against Jericho and provided the battle plan. The meeting was conducted on holy ground, a reference to the deity of the Commander, who we believe to be Jesus Christ.

Taking Jericho
Joshua 6

The Seven Trumpets of Jericho by James Jacques Joseph Tissot (1896-1902)

Israel was destined to take the promise land. They crossed the Jordan and faced Jericho.

Now Jericho was shut up inside and outside because of the people of Israel. None went out, and none came in. And the Lord said to Joshua, "See, I have given Jericho into your hand, with its king and mighty men of valor. You shall march around the city, all the men of war going around the city once. Thus, shall you do for six days. Seven priests shall bear seven trumpets of rams' horns before the ark. On the seventh day you shall march around the city seven times, and the priests shall blow the trumpets. And when they make a long blast with the ram's horn, when you hear the sound of the trumpet, then all the people shall shout with a great shout, and the wall of the city will fall down flat, and the people shall go up, everyone straight before him." So, Joshua the son of Nun called the priests and said to them, "Take up the ark of the covenant and let seven priests bear seven trumpets of rams' horns before the ark of the Lord." And he said to the people, "Go forward. March around the city and let the armed men pass on before the ark of the Lord."

This they did and the city fell.

Sun Stands Still
Joshua 10

Joshua Stops the Rotation of the Sun by Carlo Maratta (1700)

The city of Gibeon made peace with the Israelites after the taking of Jericho, so five local kings attacked Gibeon, who called for help.

So, Joshua went up from Gilgal, he and all the people of war with him, and all the mighty men of valor. And the Lord said to Joshua, "Do not fear them, for I have given them into your hands. Not a man of them shall stand before you." So, Joshua came upon them suddenly, having marched up all night from Gilgal. And the Lord threw them into a panic before Israel, who struck them with a great blow at Gibeon... And as they fled before Israel, while they were going down the ascent of Beth-horon, the Lord threw down large stones from heaven on them as far as Azekah, and they died. There were more who died because of the hailstones than the sons of Israel killed with the sword.

At that time Joshua spoke to the Lord in the day when the Lord gave the Amorites over to the sons of Israel, and he said in the sight of Israel, "Sun, stand still at Gibeon, and moon, in the Valley of Aijalon." And the sun stood still, and the moon stopped, until the nation took vengeance on their enemies.

Is this not written in the Book of Jashar? The sun stopped in the midst of heaven and did not hurry to set for about a whole day. There has been no day like it before or since, when the Lord heeded the voice of a man, for the Lord fought for Israel.

Ehud
Judges 3

Hall of Justice fresco, Ehud Kills Eglon King of the Moabites by Teofilo Torri (1608)

The Israelites did evil in the time of the judges following Joshua's death, but the Lord rescued them when seriously threatened. Such was the case with Ehud, whom the Lord raised up to confront Moab.

Eglon king of Moab gathered the Ammonites and Amalekites and defeated Israel.

Ehud, son of Gera, the Benjaminite, arranged to bring tribute to Eglon, then said he had a message for him in secret. Eglon sent his aides away. Ehud drew a special sword from his right side and thrust it into Eglon's belly, then quietly departed.

When Ehud arrived in Seirah, he sounded the trumpet, gathered the people of Israel, took the fords of the Jordan, and subdued Moab.

Deborah
Judges 4

Jael Shows to Barak, Sisera Lying Dead by James Jacques Joseph Tissot (1896-1902)

So too, the Lord raised up Deborah to judge Israel.

Jabin king of Canaan oppressed Israel, so Deborah sent Barak and the Israeli army to eliminate the Canaan army led by Sisera. Barak was successful, but Sisera escaped, seeking refuge in the supposedly friendly tent of Jael.

Jael comforted Sisera, who went to sleep. Knowing he was wanted by the Israelites, she took the opportunity to slay him, driving a tent peg into his temple while he slept. She then showed the results to Barak.

Israel will suffer because they worship false gods, but the Lord will come to their aid when needed. One day they will comprehend.

The Lord with Gideon
Judges 6-8

The Angel and Gideon by Gerbrand van den Eeckhout (1640)

Then there was Gideon. When the Midianites and Amalekites oppressed the Israelites, the Lord chose Gideon as judge to draw the tribes together and lead the nation. He found Gideon hiding from the Midianites, beating out wheat in a winepress. We believe this to be the incarnate Son of God.

Gideon tested the Lord with offerings and fleece. The Lord patiently satisfied Gideon's need for proof of the His authority.

The Lord had Gideon destroy the Altar of Baal, and then prepare an army to oppose the enemy.

Gideon gathered 32,000 men, but the Lord said he had too many, eventually whittling down the number to 300. This meager number, equipped with trumpets and jars with torches inside, assaulted the enemy encampment one night. All blew their trumpets on cue, broke the jars to reveal the light, and shouted *"For the LORD and for Gideon"* as they charged downhill. The frightened enemy scattered and were hunted down by all of Israel.

Jephthah
Judges 11

Jephthah Returning from Battle is Greeted by his Daughter by Giovanni Antonio Pellegrini (1708-1713)

Then Jephthah. The son of Gilead and a harlot, Jephthah was rejected by his family and the city until God raised him up as a mighty warrior to rescue Israel from the Ammonites. The people of Gilead asked him to lead their army, which he accepted.

And Jephthah made a vow to the Lord: "If you give the Ammonites into my hands, whatever comes out of the door of my house to meet me when I return in triumph from the Ammonites will be the Lord's, and I will sacrifice it as a burnt offering."

Jephthah was successful against the Ammonites, but what came from his door when he returned home was his beloved daughter. He regretted his foolish oath.

At the sermon on the mount, Christ instructed the people. *"You have heard it said to those of old, 'You shall not swear falsely, but shall perform to the Lord what you have sworn.' But I say to you, do not take an oath at all, either by heaven, for it is the throne of God, or by the earth, for it is His footstool, or by Jerusalem, for it is the city of the great King. And do not take an oath by your head, for you cannot make one hair white or black. "Let what you say be simply 'Yes' or 'No'; anything more than this comes from evil."* (Matthew 5)

Foretelling the Birth of Samson
Judges 13

Sacrifice of Manoah by Pieter Lastman (1624)

And Samson. The Angel of the Lord told Manoah and his wife they would have a son who would be a Nazirite (circa 1118 B.C.). When asked His name, the Angel of the Lord replied that it was Wonderful, and Manoah and his wife offered sacrifice, saying they had seen the Lord, who we believe was Jesus Christ.

In Isaiah 9 we read, *"For to us a Child is born, to us a Son is given, and the government will be on His shoulders. And He will be called Wonderful, Counselor, Mighty God, Everlasting Father, Prince of Peace."*

Samson
Judges 14

Samson and the Lion by Luca Giordano (1694-1696)

Samson fell in love with a woman of Timnah, one of the daughters of the Philistines, who ruled over Israel during this time. He asked his father to arrange the marriage.

On the way to see his bride-to-be, a lion attacked him near the vineyards. *The Spirit of the Lord rushed upon him, and although he had nothing in his hand, he tore the lion in pieces.*

Some days later, on his way to claim his bride, Samson found the lion's carcass with a swarm of bees and honey inside the body.

At the wedding feast, Samson posed a riddle to thirty companions, giving them a week to solve it. The wager was thirty linen garments and thirty changes of clothes. Riddle: *Out of the eater came something to eat. Out of the strong came something sweet.*

They had no clue and so threatened his bride they would burn her and her father's house if she did not get the riddle from Samson. He told her and in turn she told the companions, who won the wager. This enraged Samson, who went to Ashkelon, struck down thirty Philistines, and plundered their garments to honor his wager.

The story of Samson's riddle tells us that life can come through death. Christ's death and resurrection give us life.

Samson and Deliah – Betrayal
Judges 16

Samson and Delilah by Anthony van Dyck (1599-1641)

Samson then fell in love with Deliliah, a Philistine woman. Now the Philistines were a strong and great enemy of Isreal, while Samson was to them a troublemaker. So, their leaders bribed Delilah to gain Samson's trust and learn the secret of his strength. When she did, she turned him over to the authorities while he slept. They cut his hair, blinded him, and put him to work.

This act reminds us of the betrayal of Judas, who sold Christ to the authorities for thirty pieces of silver. In both cases, the betrayal led to bondage, torture, and death.

Samson's Death
Judges 16

Samson Destroys the Philistine Temple by Giovanni Benedetto Castiglione called Grechetto (17th century)

Samson was able to perform one last feat against the Philistines. They allowed his hair to regrow, forgetting it was key to his strength, and brought him to the temple of Dagon to mock him, where he caused the temple to collapse, killing many people, including himself.

How Far can Men Fall
Judges 19-21

The Levite of Ephraim by Alexandre-François Caminade (1837)

A Levite of Ephraim was traveling home after visiting with his father-in-law. He traveled with his concubine, a servant, and two donkeys.

They took lodging one night in Gibeah with an older man who offered them shelter. That night wicked men of the city surrounded the house and demanded the older man give them the visitor so they could have their way with him. The older man tried to reason with them and even offered his virgin daughter and the man's concubine instead. They would not listen. To spare himself, the Levite sent his concubine outside. They abused her all night. In the morning, she was found dead with her hands on the threshold. He loaded her onto a donkey and traveled home, where he cut her body into twelve pieces and sent them to the tribes of Israel.

The tribes tried to punish those responsible, but the Benjaminites protected the guilty resulting in a civil war that eradicated all but 600 men of the tribe. To save the tribe, they allowed these 600 to steal eligible maidens from the city of Jabesh Gilead, who did not respond when called to battle.

Men without God become evil. False gods deceive you into believing you can earn your salvation. True faith is the indwelling Holy Spirit transforming your motivations from satisfying selfish desires to serving others humbly. Read the scriptures daily.

Return to Bethlehem
Ruth 1

Ruth and Naomi by Philip Hermogenes Calderon (1833-1898)

Ruth and Elimelech left Bethlehem for Moab with their two sons because of famine. There the sons married Moabite women, Ruth and Orpah. The men all died in Moab, so Naomi decided to return to Bethlehem, encouraging her childless daughters-in-law to return home to find husbands. Orpah kissed her and made ready to return home, but Ruth clung to Naomi saying,

"Do not urge me to leave you or to return from following you. For where you go, I will go, and where you lodge, I will lodge. Your people shall be my people, and your God my God. Where you die, I will die, and there will I be buried. May the Lord do so to me and more also if anything but death parts me from you."

Naomi understood Ruth would not be dissuaded, so they journeyed to Bethlehem together.

Goel
Ruth 2-4

Ruth in Boaz's Field by Julius Schnorr von Carolsfeld (1828)

They had little in resources, so Ruth gleaned in the fields of Boaz, son of Rahab and kinsman to Naomi. Boaz loved Ruth and served as Goel, redeeming Naomi's land and fulfilling the Leverite marriage responsibilities of next of kin for Ruth. It is a wonderful story.

Ruth and Boaz were David's great-grandparents. The story is viewed as an analogy of Jesus Christ (Boaz), who redeems the land for his people, Israel (Naomi), and takes a gentile bride, the Church (Ruth).

Hannah Prays for a Son
1 Samuel 1

Hannah at Prayer by Wilhelm Wachtel (1875-1942)

Elkanah had two wives, Hannah, who was barren, and Peninnah, who was quite fertile, producing a number of sons and daughters. Peninnah would provoke Hannah grievously for many years just to irritate her.

Now Elkanah loved Hannah but he could not console her.

When they visited the Temple in Shiloh, *she was deeply distressed and prayed to the Lord and wept bitterly. And she vowed a vow and said, "O Lord of hosts, if You will indeed look on the affliction of Your servant and remember me and not forget Your servant, but will give to Your servant a son, then I will give him to the Lord all the days of his life, and no razor shall touch his head."*

The Lord heard her prayer and gave her a son, and she kept her vow, giving Samuel to the High Priest Eli when he was a child.

The Lord Speaks to Samuel
1 Samuel 3

Depiction of Eli and Samuel by John Singleton Copley (1780)

Samuel (circa 1094-1019 B.C.) prophesied for the Lord even as a boy. The first time the Lord called him as he lay in bed, he thought it was Eli. In fact, the Lord called Samuel three times before Eli realized the Lord was speaking to the boy, and so instructed him to respond appropriately. When he did, the Lord gave him this prophecy.

Then the Lord said to Samuel: *"Behold, I will do something in Israel at which both ears of everyone who hears it will tingle. In that day I will perform against Eli all that I have spoken concerning his house, from beginning to end. For I have told him that I will judge his house forever for the iniquity which he knows, because his sons made themselves vile, and he did not restrain them. And therefore, I have sworn to the house of Eli that the iniquity of Eli's house shall not be atoned for by sacrifice or offering forever."*

While Samuel was hesitant to report all of this, he consented at Eli's insistence.

Ark Taken
1 Samuel 4-6

The Plague of the Philistines at Ashdod by Pieter van Halen (1661)

Israel went to battle with the Philistines at Ebenezar and were defeated. The Israelites then called for the Ark of the Covenant to be brought from Shiloh to their camp to protect them from the Philistines, who reengaged, killing many, including the sons of Eli, and captured the Ark. When Eli was informed of this encounter, he fell, broke his neck, and died being old and heavy.

The Philistines placed the Ark in the house of their god Dagon to show his superiority, but over the following days they found Dagon toppled, decapitated, with both hands amputated found on the threshold, which is why all who enter the house of Dagon avoid stepping on the threshold to this day.

The hand of the Lord was heavy against the people of Ashdod, and He terrified and afflicted them with tumors, both Ashdod and its territory. (1 Samuel 5)

They had trouble throughout the land for seven months until they sent the Ark back to the Israelites on a newly made cart pulled by two milk cows that had never been yoked.

The Glory of the Lord was in the Ark, and He will not be mocked.

Saul as King
1 Samuel 9-15

Saul Reproved by Samuel by John Singleton Copley (1798)

The people clamored for a king, so the Lord had Samuel anoint Saul, a Benjaminite, as king. He fought many battles, but when he fought the Amalekites...

Samuel said to Saul, "The Lord sent me to anoint you king over Israel; now therefore listen to the words of the Lord. Thus says the Lord of hosts, 'I have noted what Amalek did to Israel in opposing them on the way when they came up out of Egypt. Now go and strike Amalek and devote to destruction all that they have. Do not spare them but kill both man and woman, child and infant, ox and sheep, camel and donkey.'"

But when the battle ended, he spared Agag and the best of the livestock, so the Lord rejected him as king.

Anointing David
1 Samuel 16

Anointing of David by Samuel by Felix-Joseph Barrias (1842)

King Saul lost favor with God when he failed to do as instructed, so God selected his replacement, a son of Jesse. Each son passed before Samuel, but none were selected.

And Samuel said to Jesse, "The Lord has not chosen these." Then Samuel said to Jesse, "Are all your sons here?" And he said, there remains yet the youngest, but he is keeping the sheep." And Samuel said to Jesse, "Send and get him, for we will not sit down till he comes here." And he sent and brought him in.

Now he was ruddy and had beautiful eyes and was handsome. And the Lord said, "Arise, anoint him, for this is he." Then Samuel took the horn of oil and anointed him in the midst of his brothers, and the Spirit of the Lord rushed upon David from that day forward.

Playing for the King
1 Samuel 16

David and Saul by Ernst Josephson (1878)

Now the Spirit of the Lord departed from Saul, and a harmful spirit from the Lord tormented him. And Saul's servants said to him, "Behold now, a harmful spirit from God is tormenting you. Let our lord now command your servants who are before you to seek out from the Lord a man who is skillful in playing the lyre, and when the harmful spirit from God is upon you, he will play it, and you will be well." So, Saul said to his servants, "Provide for me a man who can play well and bring him to me." One of the young men answered, "Behold, I have seen a son of Jesse the Bethlehemite, who is skillful in playing, a man of valor, a man of war, prudent in speech, and a man of good presence, and the Lord is with him." Therefore, Saul sent messengers to Jesse and said, "Send me David your son, who is with the sheep." And Jesse took a donkey laden with bread and a skin of wine and a young goat and sent them by David his son to Saul. And David came to Saul and entered his service. And Saul loved him greatly, and he became his armor-bearer. And Saul sent to Jesse, saying, "Let David remain in my service, for he has found favor in my sight." And whenever the harmful spirit from God was upon Saul, David took the lyre and played it with his hand. So, Saul was refreshed and was well, and the harmful spirit departed from him.

David and Goliath
1 Samuel 17

David Slaying Goliath by Peter Paul Rubens (1616)

Before David was old enough to join the army, he visited his brothers on the battlefield when the Israelites faced the Philistines. At the time, the Philistines were challenging the Israelites to send a champion to face Goliath, a nine-foot six-inch giant wearing 130 pounds of armor. Israel had no soldier willing to face such a warrior.

When David heard the taunt Goliath uttered against Israel, he was enraged and vowed to face Goliath himself. King Saul allowed it because of David's confidence and experience as a shepherd against lions and bears.

David approach Goliath with staff and sling saying, *I come to you in the name of the Lord of hosts, the God of the armies of Israel, whom you have defied. This day the Lord will deliver you into my hand, and I will strike you down and cut off your head. And I will give the dead bodies of the host of the Philistines this day to the birds of the air and to the wild beasts of the earth, that all the earth may know there is a God in Israel, and that all this assembly may know that the Lord saves not with sword and spear. For the battle is the Lord's, and He will give you into our hand.* Then David slung a stone at Goliath's forehead, and when he fell, David severed his head.

What a glowing example of recognizing that the battle we face is the Lord's. Surely, we do our part in believing and appropriately acting. Our greatest enemy is sin, and we believe Jesus Christ's sacrifice and resurrection was victorious and free all who believe.

Abigail
1 Samuel 25

The Wise Abigail by Luca Giordano (1696-1697)

When Saul threatened David's life, he took his men and fled. Without resources, he requested help to feed his men from Nabal, a wealthy but cruel man. Nabal refused this hero of Israel. David pondered retaliation until Abigail, Nabal's wife, intervened, providing food and drink and persuading the future king to be merciful.

David saw her as wise and married her upon her husband's death.

Like Abigail, humbleness results in mercy from the Lord.

The Witch of Endor
1 Samuel 28

Saul and the Witch of Endor by Benjamin West (1777)

Saul had no advisor that could help him understand God's direction, so he sought out a sorceress to raise the spirit of Samuel, who had advised him before his death. Such necromancy is forbidden because it disturbs the dead and seeks hidden knowledge.

Christ, the Son of God, alone can rightfully move between realms along with those with his permission.

Saul paid for his error. Samuel rebuked his behavior and told him he would soon join him in death.

Death of Saul
1 Samuel 31

Death of King Saul by Elie Zvi Marcuse (1850)

King Saul died in battle against the Philistines along with all his sons.

David severely mourned their loss. Even though Saul had sought his own death, he had once been the Lord's chosen king. And Saul's eldest son, Jonathan, with whom he shared a deep brotherly love, had warned him of the danger posed by his father.

Your glory, O Israel, is slain on your high places! How the mighty have fallen... Saul and Jonathan, beloved and lovely! In life and in death, they were not divided; they were swifter than eagles; they were stronger than lions.

Such devotion is born of the Spirit, as we find in Christ and believers.

David was subsequently anointed king.

Return of the Ark of the Covenant
1 Chronicles 15-16

David Bearing the Ark of Testament into Jerusalem by Domenico Gargiulo (1609-1675)

The Philistines captured the Ark of the Covenant in battle but sent it back because its presence caused trouble.

After a failed attempt using a cart, David had it carefully carried to Jerusalem and placed in a tent.

The people celebrated its return. The Word of God belongs with the people of God.

Rebuke, Humbleness, Forgiveness
2 Samuel 11-12

The Prophet Nathan Rebukes King David by Eugène Siberdt (1866-1931)

King David slept with his neighbor Bathsheba, who became pregnant. David recalled her husband, Uriah, from war so the pregnancy could be thought of as his. When he arrived, he refused to go to his wife while his men were in combat, so David sent him back and arranged for him to die in battle, then he married Bathsheba. The prophet Nathan, David's advisor, confronted him:

Why have you despised the word of the Lord, to do what is evil in His sight? You have struck down Uriah the Hittite with the sword and have taken his wife to be your wife and have killed him with the sword of the Ammonites. Now therefore the sword shall never depart from your house, because you have despised me and have taken the wife of Uriah the Hittite to be your wife.' Thus says the Lord, 'Behold, I will raise up evil against you out of your own house. And I will take your wives before your eyes and give them to your neighbor, and he shall lie with your wives in the sight of this sun. For you did it secretly, but I will do this thing before all Israel and before the sun.'" David said to Nathan, "I have sinned against the Lord." And Nathan said to David, "The Lord also has put away your sin; you shall not die. Nevertheless, because by this deed you have utterly scorned the Lord, the child who is born to you shall die.

David suffered consequences for his actions, which he recognized as evil and repented, humbling himself. And God forgave him as he does the whole world through Christ our Lord and Savior.

David's Census Brings Pestilence
1 Chronicles 21

Appearance of the Angel to King David by Luca Giordano (1634-1705)

David's census displeased the Lord, so he sent a pestilence on Israel and 70,000 fell; then he sent the Angel of the Lord to destroy Jerusalem. David (1040-970 B.C.) lifted his eyes and saw the Angel of the Lord between heaven and earth. He fell on his face and prayed, and the Lord was merciful.

Absalom's Death
2 Samuel 13-19

The Death of Absalom woven in 1817 at the Royal Tapestry Factory in Madrid, under the guidance of its director, Don Livinio Stuyck y Vandergoten

David had many wives and children. His eldest son, Amnon, fell in love with his half-sister, Tamar, raped, and discarded her. Her brother, Absalom, David's favorite, counseled her to reject vengeance, then plotted to kill Amnon through deception.

He fled afterwards but returned to seize the crown. In the ensuing battle, Absalom fled again by horseback but was caught by his flowing hair in a forest tree. Pursuing forces pierced him ending his life, against David's wishes.

This death foreshadows Christ; anyone hung in a tree is cursed; and sin is slain.

Succession
1 Kings 1-2

Bathsheba's Appeal to David by Govert Flinck (1651)

Adonijah, David's son with Haggith, had himself declared king when David was very old. Upon hearing this, Bathsheba came to David, while Abishag the Shunammite was attending to him, and paid homage saying,

My lord, you swore to your servant by the Lord your God, saying, 'Solomon your son shall reign after me, and he shall sit on my throne.' And now, behold, Adonijah is king, although you, my lord the king, do not know it.

David immediately had Bathsheba's son, Solomon, declared king, which caused Adonijah to withdraw in fear and pay homage to Solomon.

The Lord had already chosen Solomon to be king after him. (1 Chronicles 28)

Solomon forgave his older half-brother. However, he had him put to death after he requested Abishag.

My Servant
Psalm 22 - Isaiah 53

Christ on the Cross Between the Two by Peter Paul Rubens (1620)

These scriptural references were written hundreds of years before Jesus Christ, yet read as though written from the cross.

Excerpts:

My God, My God, why have You abandoned me...I am a worm, less than human; scorned by men, despised by people...Dogs surround Me; a pack of evil ones closes in on Me, like lions they maul My hands and feet...I take count of all My bones while they look on and gloat...They divide My clothes among themselves, casting lots for My garments.

Yet it was our sickness that He was bearing, our suffering that He endured. We accounted Him plagued, smitten and afflicted by God; but He was wounded because of our sins, crushed because of our iniquities. He bore the chastisement that made us whole, and by His bruises we were healed.

He knows the end from the beginning and does nothing that He hasn't told His prophets (Amos 3:7). It was written before it came to pass.

The Lord Grants Solomon Wisdom
2 Chronicles 1

Solomon's Dream by Luca Giordano (1693)

After David's death, Solomon reigned as king (circa 970-931 B.C.). The Lord asked Solomon what gift he desired, and because Solomon asked for wisdom, the Lord also gave him wealth and honor.

The Judgement of Solomon – Sacrifice
1 Kings 3

The Judgement of Solomon by Mattias Stom (1640)

Two pregnant harlots delivered babies only days apart. One of the children died, and his mother switched him with the live child that evening when the household was sleeping.

When his mother awoke, she realized the child was not hers and took her grievance to King Solomon.

Faced with two women who claimed to be the child's parent, the king decided to give them each half. This satisfied the dead baby's mother but the true mother was aghast, so she agreed to give the child away. The king then knew the true mother.

Many ask where is Christ in this story? I suggest you think about the lesson. The true mother was willing to sacrifice her happiness to do what was best to save her child just as Christ sacrificed His happiness, even His life, for you. You must be of great value!

Solomon's Temple
1 Kings 6 - 2 Chronicles 3

The Queen of Sheba Before the Temple of Solomon in Jerusalem by Salomon de Bray (1597-1664)

Solomon's temple replaced the tabernacle (circa 970 B.C.). Besides being larger, the temple included two large columns, named Jachin (Yah establishes) and Boaz (strength), and side closets for the priests' personal items (perhaps representing hidden sin).

The glory of the Lord left the first temple, described by Ezekiel (circa 590 B.C.) and Nebuchadnezzar destroyed it (circa 586 B.C,). The second temple was built in the time of Ezra (circa 515 B.C.), which was renovated and expanded by Herod the Great (circa 10 B.C.). This was the temple Jesus visited.

The New Testament identifies believers as the temple of God, because His Spirit resides in us.

All is Vanity
Ecclesiastes

Vanity of Vanities and All is Vanity by Isaac Asknaziy (19th Century)

King Solomon wrote Ecclesiastes which began… *The words of the Preacher, the son of David, king in Jerusalem. Vanity of vanities, says the Preacher, vanity of vanities! All is vanity.*

Solomon explains the activities we pursue in life and how they mean nothing because all is vanity. You have the famous lines… *For everything there is a season, and a time for every matter under heaven: a time to be born, and a time to die…* yet all is vanity.

Solomon finishes… *The end of the matter; all has been heard. Fear God and keep his commandments, for this is the whole duty of man. For God will bring every deed into judgment, with every secret thing, whether good or evil.*

True enough, but the law is insufficient, its protection is temporary, which is why the Father sent us Christ.

The King's Love
Song of Solomon

The Shunamite Relating the Glories of King Solomon to Her Maidens by Albert Joseph Moore (1894)

Here we have the love story between King Solomon and his Shulammite bride, an intimate description of passion, care, and devotion of both body and spirit.

My bride, my true love, a garden enclosed; hedged all about, a fountain shut in and sealed! What wealth of grace is here! (4:12)

Does this not foreshadow the love Christ, the King of kings, has for the church?

Husbands, love your wives, as Christ loved the church and gave Himself up for her, that He might sanctify her, having cleansed her by the washing of water with the word, so He might present the church to Himself in splendor, without spot or wrinkle or any such thing, that she might be holy and without blemish. (Ephesians 5:25-27)

Sad Ending
1 Kings 11

King Solomon's Idolatry by Giovanni Venanzi di Pesaro (1668)

Where did Solomon's wisdom lead him?

He had 700 wives, who were princesses, and 300 concubines. And his wives turned away his heart. For when Solomon was old, his wives turned away his heart after other gods, and his heart was not wholly true to the Lord his God, as was the heart of David his father. For Solomon went after Ashtoreth, the goddess of the Sidonians, and after Milcom, the abomination of the Ammonites. So, Solomon did what was evil in the sight of the Lord and did not wholly follow the Lord, as David his father had done.

Therefore, the Lord said to Solomon, "Since this has been your practice and you have not kept My covenant and My statutes that I have commanded you, I will surely tear the kingdom from you and will give it to your servant. Yet for the sake of David, your father I will not do it in your days, but I will tear it out of the hand of your son. However, I will not tear away all the kingdom, but I will give one tribe to your son, for the sake of David My servant and for the sake of Jerusalem that I have chosen."

Do you consider yourself wise? Might we have the need for Jesus the Christ?

Division of the Kingdom
1 Kings 12

Jeroboam Offering Sacrifice for the Idol by Jean-Honoré Fragonard (1752)

Solomon's son, Rehoboam, of the house of Judah, abused the people so the kingdom split. Ten tribes followed Jeroboam, who became the first king of the Northern Kingdom.

He too was an evil ruler (all were in the North), leading the Northern Kingdom into idolatry, because he was concerned the people would return to Jerusalem.

And Jeroboam said in his heart, "Now the kingdom will turn back to the house of David. If this people go up to offer sacrifices in the temple of the Lord at Jerusalem, then the heart of this people will turn again to their lord, to Rehoboam king of Judah, and they will kill me and return to Rehoboam king of Judah." So, the king took counsel and made two calves of gold. And he said to the people, "You have gone up to Jerusalem long enough. Behold your gods, O Israel, who brought you up out of the land of Egypt."

Consequences of Idolatry
1 Kings 14

Jeroboam's Wife and Prophet Ahija by Ludovico Venuti (1822)

When Jeroboam's son fell ill, the king sent his wife disguised to the Prophet Ahijah, who prophesized Jeroboam would be king.

When the old, blind prophet heard her coming, he said…

"Come in, wife of Jeroboam. Why do you pretend to be another? For I am charged with unbearable news for you. Go, tell Jeroboam, 'Thus says the Lord, the God of Israel: "Because I exalted you from among the people and made you leader over My people Israel and tore the kingdom away from the house of David and gave it to you, and yet you have not been like My servant David, who kept My commandments and followed Me with all his heart, doing only that which was right in My eyes, but you have done evil above all who were before you and have gone and made for yourself other gods and metal images, provoking Me to anger, and have cast Me behind your back, therefore behold, I will bring harm upon the house of Jeroboam and will cut off from Jeroboam every male, both bond and free in Israel, and will burn up the house of Jeroboam, as a man burns up dung until it is all gone…' Arise therefore, go to your house. When your feet enter the city, the child shall die."

There is a price to pay for wrongdoing, and in the end, it was paid by Christ for all.

Raised from the Dead
1 Kings 17 – Luke 7

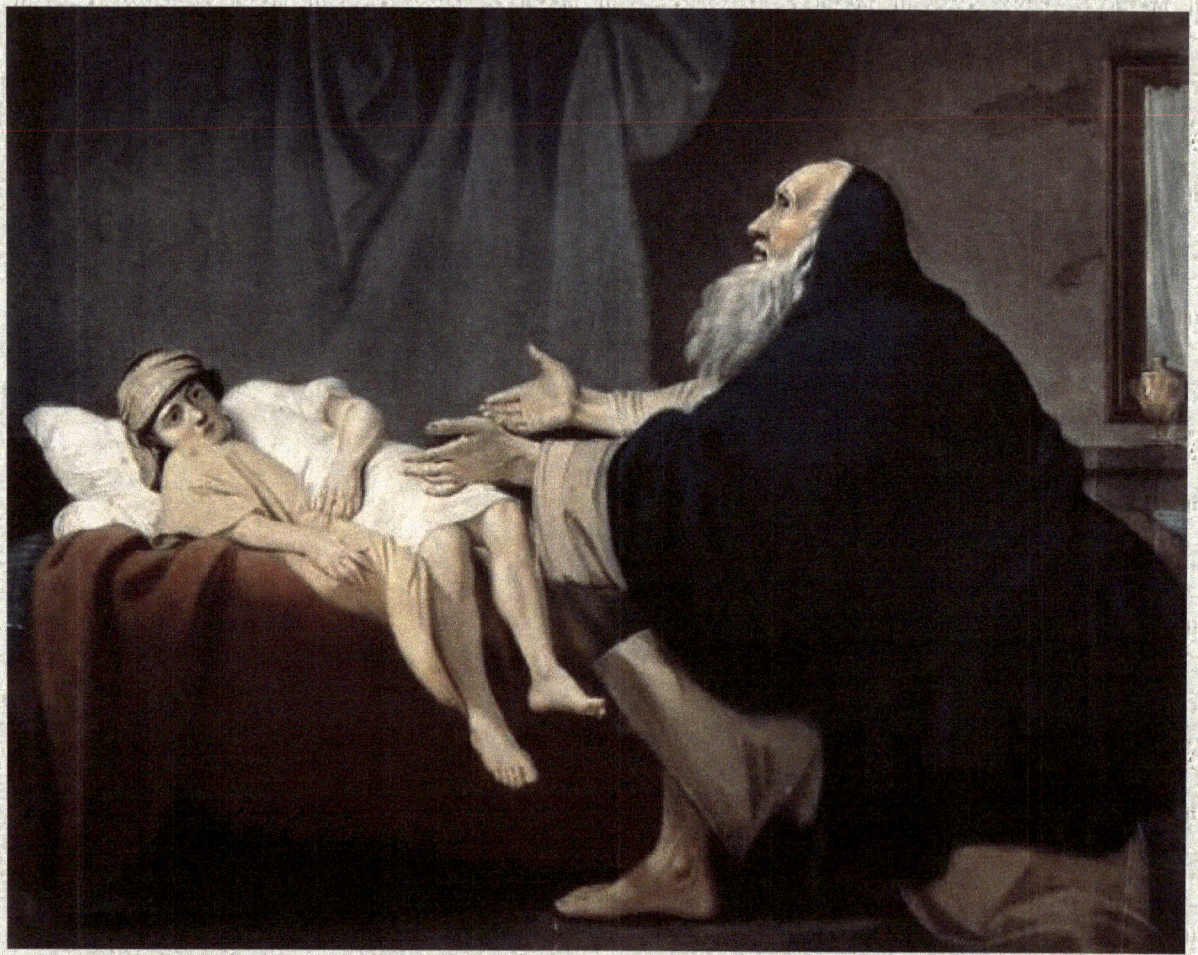

Elijah Raises the Widow's Son by Benjamin West. Colorized by Valentine Green (1799)

During Elijah's stay with the widow of Zarephath, her son became ill and died. She blamed Elijah who petitioned the Lord for his life. When he revived, Elijah returned him to his mother. This foreshadowed Christ's similar act in the town of Nain.

Accepting the Sacrifice
1 Kings 18

The Sacrifice of Elijah Before the Priests of Baal by Domenico Fetti (1621-1622)

Elijah predicted a drought in the Northern Kingdom that would last three years, and it happened. The Lord told Elijah He would bring it to an end when Elijah confronted King Ahab.

Ahab sent to all the people of Israel and gathered the prophets together at Mount Carmel. And Elijah came near to all the people and said, "How long will you go limping between two different opinions? If the Lord is God, follow Him; but if Baal, then follow him." And the people did not answer him a word.

So, Elijah set a contest between himself and the 450 prophets of Baal.

Let two bulls be given to us, and let them choose one bull for themselves and cut it in pieces and lay it on the wood, but put no fire to it. And I will prepare the other bull and lay it on the wood and put no fire to it. And you call upon the name of your god, and I will call upon the name of the Lord, and the God who answers by fire, he is God." And all the people answered, "It is well spoken."

Baal failed to answer, but God sent fire from heaven for Elijah! Then he had the false prophets of Baal slaughtered.

Power of God Came Upon Him
1 Kings 18

Elijah Running in Front of King Ahab's Chariot Towards Jezreel by Jean-Baptiste Despax (1710-1773)

After the contest with the 450 prophets of Baal…

Elijah said to Ahab, "Go up, eat and drink, for there is a sound of the rushing of rain." So, Ahab went up to eat and to drink. And Elijah went up to the top of Mount Carmel. And he bowed himself down on the earth and put his face between his knees. And he said to his servant, "Go up now, look toward the sea." And he went up and looked and said, "There is nothing." And he said, "Go again," seven times. And at the seventh time he said, "Behold, a little cloud like a man's hand is rising from the sea." And he said, "Go up, say to Ahab, 'Prepare your chariot and go down, lest the rain stop you.'" And in a little while the heavens grew black with clouds and wind, and there was a great rain. And Ahab rode and went to Jezreel. And the hand of the Lord was on Elijah, and he gathered up his garment and ran before Ahab to the entrance of Jezreel.

The power of the Lord came upon Elijah as he outran Ahab's chariot to Jezreel, much like the supernatural ability seen in Christ calming the storm (Matthew 8) or His walk on water (Matthew 14).

The Angel of the Lord with Elijah
1 Kings 19

An Angel Awakens the Prophet Elijah by Juan Antonio Frias y Escalante (1667)

The prophet Elijah was a mighty defender of Yahweh during the time of Ahab and Jezebel in the Northern Kingdom (circa 853-674 B.C.).

Jezebel was enraged by Elijah's slaughter of her prophets and threatened to kill him, so he flees to Beersheba in Judah. There, alone in the wilderness, Elijah sits under a shrub, prays for death, and falls asleep.

The Angel of the Lord brings bread and water and gently awakens Elijah, encouraging him to refresh himself. The Angel visits a second time telling him to prepare for the long journey ahead. God is not done with this devoted prophet.

Naboth's Vineyard
1 Kings 21

Jezebel by Harold Copping (1863-1932)

King Ahab desired the nearby vineyard of Naboth, but he refuse to trade or sell, so Ahab returned home to pout in his bed.

His wife, Jezebel inquired why he was so depressed. He explained the situation. Jezebel told him to not worry, then she arranged for Naboth's death.

When he went to take possession of the land, he was met by Elijah, who prophesized none of his sons would live and Jezebel would be eaten by dogs.

Ahab was an evil king but he repented of this evil deed, which resulted in mercy from the Lord.

Elijah's Ascension
2 Kings 2

Elijah Taken Up in a Chariot of Fire by Giuseppe Angeli (1740)

Having devoted his entire life to God's service in combating the evil of the Northern Kingdom of Israel, Elijah was spectacularly brought to heaven in a fiery chariot while with his loyal companion, Elisha, foreshadowing the ascension of Christ.

He would much later appear to Christ with Moses on the Mount of Transfiguration.

Dividing the Waters
2 Kings 2

Elisha Dividing the Waters of Jordan with Elijah's Mantle by Jean-Baptiste Despax (1710-1773)

When Elijah departed, he left his cloak for Elisha.

(Elisha) *took hold of his own clothes and tore them in two pieces. And he took up the cloak of Elijah that had fallen from him and went back and stood on the bank of the Jordan... and struck the water, saying, "Where is the Lord, the God of Elijah?" And... the waters parted to the one side and to the other, and Elisha went over.*

God gave Moses the same power to part the Red Sea, and Joshua parted the Jordan when the Israelites crossed. Christ, on the other hand, walked on water.

Healing the Stew
2 Kings 4

The Prophet Elisha by Giorgio Vasari (1566)

Elisha came again to Gilgal when there was a famine in the land. And as the sons of the prophets were sitting before him, he said to his servant, "Set on the large pot, and boil stew for the sons of the prophets." One of them went out into the field to gather herbs, and found a wild vine and gathered from it his lap full of wild gourds, and came and cut them up into the pot of stew, not knowing what they were. And they poured out some for the men to eat. But while they were eating of the stew, they cried out, "O man of God, there is death in the pot!" And they could not eat it. He said, "Then bring flour." And he threw it into the pot and said, "Pour some out for the men, that they may eat." And there was no harm in the pot.

Elisha made the stew clean, healing the sons of the prophets, just as Christ healed many.

Namaan's Healing
2 Kings 5

Elisha Refuses the Gifts of Namaan by Ferdinand Bol (1661)

Namaan was commander of the Syrian army who unfortunately contracted leprosy. Hearing there was a prophet in Isreal who could heal him, he set out to find him with many gifts, and was eventually sent to the home of Elisha.

Elisha sent his servant to tell Namaan to wash in the Jordan seven times and he would be healed, but Namaan was angry that Elisha didn't make a spectacle of the cure, so he left.

His servants pleaded with him to humble himself and follow the prophet's direction, which he did, and he was healed.

Namaan returned to Elisha to shower him with gifts, which Elisha refused.

So too we are healed by Christ for no cost, simply by humbling ourselves and accepting the gift.

Queen Athaliah – King Joash
2 Kings 11 – 2 Chronicles 22-23

Proclaiming Joash King by Edward Bird RA (1815)

When Athaliah, the mother of King Ahaziah saw that her son was dead, she arose and destroyed all the royal family. But Jehosheba, the daughter of King Joram, sister of Ahaziah, took Joash, the son of Ahaziah and stole him away from among the king's sons who were being put to death... and hid him from Athaliah... He remained with her six years, hidden in the house of the Lord, while Athaliah reigned over the land. In the seventh year, Jehoiada the priest sent and brought the captains of the Carites and of the guards, and had them come to him in the house of the Lord, and he showed them the king's son...

They arranged to protect Joash, now seven, and proclaim him king. When Athaliah heard the noise of this announcement, she rushed to the house of the Lord, tore her clothes, and declared all present traitors. Jehoiada the priest commanded the captains who were set over the army to take her into custody, remove her from the house of the Lord, and put her to death. This they did. Thus, the Lord preserved the generational line to Joseph, the legal, earthly father of the Messiah.

Note: Ahaziah, Joash, and his son Amaziah are omitted from Matthew's genealogical list of Judah's kingly line apparently due to their relationship to Athaliah and her father, Ahab, the idolatrous king of Israel, for God said he would visit the iniquity of the fathers on the children to the third and fourth generation. (Exodus 20:5)

Raised from the Dead
2 Kings 13

The Miracle at the Grave of Elisha by Jan Nagel (1596)

When Elijah was about to depart in a fiery chariot, he asked Elisha what he desired. A double portion of your spirit he replied, and a double portion he received.

He spent the remainder of his life serving as God's prophet to the Northern Kingdom as Elijah did before him, and he was laid to rest.

As the local residents were about to bury another in the same graveyard, they were sent scattering by a roving band of Moabite invaders, so they hastily threw the man's body into Elisha's grave. When the man's body touched Elisha's bones, he revived and stood on his feet.

How reminiscent of the raising of the dead through Christ.

Immanuel
Isaiah 7

Adoration of the Shepherds by Gerard van Honthorst (1622)

When Ahaz, king of the house of Judah, was concerned about attacks from the Northern Kingdom and Syria, the Lord assured Ahaz through Isaiah, even to the point of asking Ahaz to choose a sign, so the Lord could prove His assurance. Ahaz refused, so Isaiah spoke:

Therefore, the Lord Himself will give you a sign. Behold, the virgin shall conceive and bear a Son, and shall call His name Immanuel. He shall eat curds and honey when He knows how to refuse the evil and choose the good. For before the boy knows how to refuse the evil and choose the good, the land whose two kings you dread will be deserted.

Immanuel means God with Us.

Cast Down
Isaiah 14 – Ezekiel 28

The Fallen Angel by Alexandre Cabanel (1847)

How you are fallen from heaven, O Day Star, son of Dawn! How you are cut down to the ground, you who laid the nations low! You said in your heart, 'I will ascend to heaven; above the stars of God I will set my throne on high; I will sit on the mount of assembly in the far reaches of the north; I will ascend above the heights of the clouds; I will make myself like the Most High.' But you are brought down to Sheol, to the far reaches of the pit.

You were the signet of perfection, full of wisdom and perfect in beauty. You were in Eden, the garden of God; every precious stone was your covering, sardius, topaz, and diamond, beryl, onyx, and jasper, sapphire, emerald, and carbuncle; and crafted in gold were your settings and your engravings. On the day that you were created they were prepared. You were an anointed guardian cherub. I placed you; you were on the holy mountain of God; in the midst of the stones of fire you walked. You were blameless in your ways from the day you were created, till unrighteousness was found in you. In the abundance of your trade, you were filled with violence in your midst, and you sinned; so I cast you as a profane thing from the mountain of God, and I destroyed you, O guardian cherub, from the midst of the stones of fire. Your heart was proud because of your beauty; you corrupted your wisdom for the sake of your splendor. I cast you to the ground.

We are all capable of being blindly self-centered. Thank you, Father, for your guidance.

Leviathan
Isaiah 26-27

The Destruction of Leviathan from Doré's English Bible (1866)

Have you noticed fewer people over time profess a Christian perspective? The number of Christians worldwide is continually declining. We were warned many years ago, but few heeded the warnings.

Come, my people, enter your chambers, and shut your door behind you; hide yourselves for a little while until the fury has passed by. For behold, the Lord is coming out from His place to punish the inhabitants of the earth for their iniquity, and the earth will disclose the blood shed on it, and will no longer cover its slain.

In that day the Lord with His hard and great and strong sword will punish Leviathan the fleeing serpent, Leviathan the twisting serpent, and He will slay the dragon that is in the sea.

You may want to pay attention. Jesus is coming, we think, sometime in the near future.

Healing the Blind
Isaiah 35

Christ Healing the Blind Man by Gioacchino Assereto (1640)

God told us…

He will come and save you. Then the eyes of the blind shall be opened…

And so, He did. Jesus healed the blind.

Healing the Lame
Isaiah 35

He Heals the Lame by James Jacques Joseph Tissot (1886-1894)

And He healed the lame…

…then shall the lame man leap like a deer…

The Angel of the Lord Destroys the Assyrians
Isaiah 37

Battle of Sennacherib by Tanzio da Varallo (1629-1630)

Sennacherib, King of Assyria, invaded Judah and laid siege to Jerusalem. Hezekiah (circa 715-686 B.C.), King of Judah, petitioned the Lord for salvation. The Angel of the Lord struck down a hundred and eighty-five thousand soldiers one night, and Sennacherib returned to Nineveh.

Sent
Isaiah 48

God the Father and the Holy Spirit by Pompeo Batoni (1740-1743)

Listen to Me, O Jacob, and Israel, whom I called! I am He; I am the first, and I am the last. My hand laid the foundation of the earth, and My right hand spread out the heavens; when I call to them, they stand forth together...

Draw near to Me, hear this: from the beginning I have not spoken in secret, from the time it came to be I have been there. And now the Lord God has sent Me, and his Spirit...

And who do you imagine is speaking?

Speaking Plainly
Isaiah 61 – Luke 4

Jesus Unrolls the Book in the Synagogue by James Jacques Joseph Tissot (1886 – 1894)

Jesus' first public act after 40 days in the wilderness battling Satan…

And He came to Nazareth, where He had been brought up. And as was His custom, he went to the synagogue on the Sabbath day, and He stood up to read. And the scroll of the prophet Isaiah was given to Him. He unrolled the scroll and found the place where it was written,

"The Spirit of the Lord is upon Me, because He has anointed Me to proclaim good news to the poor. He has sent Me to proclaim liberty to the captives and recovering of sight to the blind, to set at liberty those who are oppressed, to proclaim the year of the Lord's favor."

And He rolled up the scroll and gave it back to the attendant and sat down. And the eyes of all in the synagogue were fixed on Him. And He began to say to them, "Today this Scripture has been fulfilled in your hearing."

He spoke plainly telling them He was the Messiah, from a prophet who wrote hundreds of years earlier. They were so angry, they tried to throw Him off a cliff.

When reading this scripture, He left off the next phrase, *and the day of vengeance of our God.* That day will surely come because of such response!

King Manasseh
2 Kings 21 – 2 Chronicles 33

King Manasseh in Exile by Maarten de Vos (1603)

Manasseh was twelve years old when he began to reign, and he reigned fifty-five years in Jerusalem. He did what was evil in the sight of the Lord, according to the abominations of the nations whom the Lord drove out before the people of Israel. For he rebuilt the high places that his father Hezekiah had broken down, and he erected altars to the Baals, and made Asheroth, and worshiped all the host of heaven and served them... he burned his sons as an offering in the Valley of the Son of Hinnom, and used fortune-telling and omens and sorcery, and dealt with mediums and with necromancers. He did much evil in the sight of the Lord, provoking him to anger... Manasseh led Judah and the inhabitants of Jerusalem astray...

The Lord spoke to Manasseh and to his people, but they paid no attention. Therefore, the Lord brough upon them the commanders of the army of the King of Assyria, who captured Manasseh with hooks and bound him with chains of bronze and brought him to Babylon. And when he was in distress, he entreated the favor of the Lord his God and humbled himself greatly before the God of his fathers. He prayed to Him, and God was moved by his entreaty and heard his plea and brought him again to Jerusalem into his kingdom. Then Manasseh knew that the Lord was God.

The Lord is eager to accept all those who humble themselves, and he provided the sacrificial death of Jesus Christ as payment for their sin.

The Last Good King
2 Chronicles 34-35

The Death of King Josiah by Antonio Zanchi (1660)

Josiah, grandson of Manasseh, was the last of the few good kings of Judah. He died confronting Pharaoh Neco of Egypt who was headed to attack the king of Assyria. We don't understand Josiah's interference.

Proper worship of Yahweh was reestablished under Josiah's leadership. The Book of the Law was discovered by the high priest Hilkiah while the temple was under repair. This disturbed Josiah greatly because previous kings had not kept the Word, so he sought the counsel of the wise prophetess Huldah.

She responded with words from the Lord promising curses would descend on Israel, but to the king He said, *because your heart was tender and you humbled yourself before God when you heard His words against this place and its inhabitants, and you have humbled yourself before Me and have torn your clothes and wept before Me, I also have heard you, declares the Lord. Behold, I will gather you to your fathers, and you shall be gathered to your grave in peace, and your eyes shall not see all the disaster that I will bring upon this place and its inhabitants.*

Humility goes a long way.

The Scribe
Jeremiah 17-18

The Prophets Jeremiah and Baruch by Rutilio Manetti (1600-1639)

Baruch served as Jeremiah's scribe, writing down all the words the Lord had told him.

Thus says the Lord: Take care for the sake of your lives, and do not bear a burden on the Sabbath day or bring it in by the gates of Jerusalem. And do not carry a burden out of your houses on the Sabbath or do any work, but keep the Sabbath day holy, as I commanded your fathers. Yet they did not listen or incline their ear, but stiffened their neck, that they might not hear and receive instruction.

The Sabbath day is a day of rest. It is kept every week, and has been for thousands of years. It foreshadows Christ, who is our rest. (Hebrews 4) And…

The word that came to Jeremiah from the Lord: "Arise, and go down to the potter's house, and there I will let you hear My words." So, I went down to the potter's house, and there he was working at his wheel. And the vessel he was making of clay was spoiled in the potter's hand, and he reworked it into another vessel, as it seemed good to the potter to do. Then the word of the Lord came to me: "O house of Israel, can I not do with you as this potter has done? declares the Lord. Behold, like the clay in the potter's hand, so are you in My hand, O house of Israel…"

The Lord gave us free will, but most do not listen, so He molds the events of our lives to encourage us to do well. We fail, which is why we need Christ.

Weeping Prophet
Jeramiah 31

The Prophet Jeremiah Prophesies the Fall of Jerusalem to King Zedekiah by Joseph Stallaert (1825-1903)

Jeremiah was known as the weeping prophet. He served during the time of the last four kings of Judah, Zedekiah being the last. During his time, Israel was on the decline. The Northern Kingdom of Israel had been taken by the Assyrians and the Southern Kingdom of Judah was about to be taken into captivity by the Babylonians because they would not heed Jeremiah's warnings but listened to false prophets. Jeremiah reported God's message when they were sent into captivity, telling them to peacefully endure their time in that foreign land because in seventy years they would return. He also gave them a message for the distant future.

Behold, the days are coming, declares the Lord, when I will make a new covenant with the house of Israel and the house of Judah, not like the covenant that I made with their fathers on the day when I took them by the hand to bring them out of the land of Egypt, My covenant that they broke, though I was their husband, declares the Lord. For this is the covenant that I will make with the house of Israel after those days, declares the Lord: I will put My law within them, and I will write it on their hearts. And I will be their God, and they shall be My people. And no longer shall each one teach his neighbors and each his brother, saying, 'Know the Lord,' for they shall all know Me, from the least of them to the greatest, declares the Lord. For I will forgive their iniquity, and I will remember their sin no more.

This covenant is made possible by the sacrificial death and resurrection of Jesus Christ and will take full effect during his millennial reign.

Babylonian Captivity
2 Chronicles 36

The Flight of the Prisoners by James Jacques Joseph Tissot (1896-1902)

The wrath of the Lord finally came against the Kingdom of Judah because the people failed to keep His law and fulfill the required Sabbaths for the land.

The Lord directed them to sow and harvest for six years and then let the land rest during the seventh year. After doing this seven times, the following year, the 50th, would be a Year of Jubilee. Many rules governed that year, including freedom of slaves, forgiveness of debts, and return of land sold to the original owner. They failed to keep the Sabbaths for 490 years, which meant they would be in bondage for 70 years. (Leviticus 25)

The king of the Chaldeans invaded Judah, killed the young men, plundered Jerusalem, and took many into exile into Babylon.

The Mission
Jonah 1-3

Jonah and the Whale by Pieter Lastman (1621)

The Lord called the prophet Jonah (circa 785 B.C.) to preach to the wicked city of Ninevah, which He intended to destroy. Jonah's hatred for the nation caused him to refuse, flee to Jaffa, and set sail for the distant land of Tarshish.

En route, an unusual storm beset the ship. Seeking the cause, the crew cast lots which identified Jonah as the source. He confirms his guilt and tells them the storm would end if they throw him overboard. They are hesitant but eventually comply.

The storm ends while Jonah is swallowed by a great fish.

Jonah, suffering in the belly for three days and three nights, immerses himself in prayer and thanksgiving, paying homage to the Lord, who then commands the fish to vomit him out on dry land.

The Lord repeats His command to preach to Ninevah and Jonah obeys. Those in the city harken to his warning and change their ways, saving the city from destruction.

Jesus Christ was in the grave three days and three nights, and if you harken to His voice, you will be saved.

Gospel Message
Jonah 3-4

Jonah Under His Gourd by Maarten van Heemskerck (1561)

After Jonah went through the city barking *"Yet forty days, and Nineveh shall be overthrown!"* and the people repented, Jonah left the city to the east, built a shelter, and angrily stewed about the Lord's compassion for the city.

Now the Lord God appointed a plant and made it come up over Jonah, that it might be a shade over his head, to save him from his discomfort. So, Jonah was exceedingly glad because of the plant. But when dawn came up the next day, God appointed a worm that attacked the plant, so that it withered.

This was not an ordinary worm. The Hebrew word is tola, a crimson worm that attaches itself to a tree, lays its eggs, protects and nourishes its offspring with its own body until it dies.

This represents Christ, who came to replace the law (the plant), which was given by God as temporary protection for man, who could not keep it.

The law was replaced by grace, secured through faith, which the accompanying, indwelling Holy Spirit employs to adapt our thoughts and actions to conform to God's ways.

The Glory of the Lord
Ezekiel 1

The Vision of the Prophet Ezekiel by Ditlev Blunck (1830)

Ezekiel (circa 622-570 B.C.) - *As I looked, behold, a stormy wind came out of the north, and a great cloud, with brightness around it, and fire flashing forth continually, and in the midst of the fire, as it were gleaming metal. And from the midst of it came the likeness of four living creatures... And above the expanse over their heads there was the likeness of a throne, in appearance like sapphire; and seated above the likeness of a throne was a likeness with a human appearance... Such was the appearance of the likeness of the glory of the Lord. And when I saw it, I fell on my face, and I heard the voice of one speaking.*

Valley of Dry Bones
Ezekiel 37

The Vision of Ezekiel by Francisco Collantes (1630)

The hand of the Lord was upon me, and He brought me out in the Spirit of the Lord and set me down in the middle of the valley; it was full of bones... And He said to me, "Prophesy over these bones, and say to them, O dry bones, hear the word of the Lord. Thus says the Lord God to these bones: Behold, I will cause breath to enter you, and you shall live. And I will lay sinews upon you, and will cause flesh to come upon you, and cover you with skin, and put breath in you, and you shall live, and you shall know that I am the Lord."

Then He said to me, "Son of man, these bones are the whole house of Israel. Behold, they say, 'Our bones are dried up, and our hope is lost; we are indeed cut off.' Therefore prophesy, and say to them, thus says the Lord God: Behold, I will open your graves and raise you from your graves, O My people. And I will bring you into the land of Israel. And you shall know that I am the Lord, when I open your graves, and raise you from your graves, O My people. And I will put My Spirit within you, and you shall live, and I will place you in your own land. Then you shall know that I am the Lord; I have spoken, and I will do it, declares the Lord."

Israel became a nation in May of 1948, so this prophecy has been partially fulfilled, but graves did not open. One day they will. *For the Lord himself will descend from heaven with a cry of command, with the voice of an archangel, and with the sound of the trumpet of God. And the dead in Christ will rise first.* (1 Thessalonians 4)

Gog
Ezekiel 38

God's Judgment upon Gog by Asher Brown Durand (1851-1852)

Thus says the Lord God: Behold, I am against you, O Gog, chief prince of Meshech and Tubal. And I will turn you about and put hooks into your jaws, and I will bring you out, and all your army.... Persia, Cush, and Put are with them, all of them, with shield and helmet; Gomer and all his hordes; Beth-togarmah from the uttermost parts of the north with all his hordes—many peoples are with you.

In the latter years you will go against the land that is restored from war... Israel...

Thus says the Lord God: On that day, thoughts will come into your mind, and you will devise an evil scheme and say, 'I will go up against the land of unwalled villages. I will fall upon the quiet people who dwell securely, all of them dwelling without walls, and having no bars or gates,' to seize spoil and carry off plunder...

I will summon a sword against Gog on all My mountains, declares the Lord God. Every man's sword will be against his brother. With pestilence and bloodshed, I will enter into judgment with him, and I will rain upon him and his hordes and the many peoples who are with him torrential rains and hailstones, fire and sulfur.

Who is this Gog? In the Septuagint translation, Amos 7 identifies Gog as the king of the locusts. In Revelation 9 this king is the angel of the bottomless pit. His name in Hebrew is Abaddon, and in Greek he is called Apollyon.

Kingdoms of the World
Daniel 2

Daniel before Nebuchadnezzar by Salomon (de) Koninck (1609 – 1656)

King Nebuchadnezzar was disturbed by a dream. He required his wise men to know and interpret the dream, but they could not. Daniel, who was a captive from Israel, told the King that his God could provide the explanation he desired.

Daniel explained that the dream was of an image that represented the successive empires of the world, beginning with Nebuchadnezzar as the head of gold, to be followed by the Media-Persian Empire, the Greek empire, the Roman Empire, and a dissolved Roman empire, which would be broken by a stone from heaven, who is Jesus Christ. It was all written before completed, so you would know He sent it.

The Fiery Furnace
Daniel 3

Shadrach, Meshach and Abednego in the Furnace by Luca Giordano (1705)

Nebuchadnezzar erected a gold statue of himself and required everyone to bow down to it.

Now there were young men who had been taken captive with Daniel named Hananiah, Mishael, and Azariah who had been renamed Shadrach, Meshach, and Abednego in Babylon.

These young men refused to bow down to the image of Nebuchadnezzar, so the king had them thrown into a fiery furnace.

Nebuchadnezzar was amazed when he observed these men, untouched by the heat or flames, walking unbound in the fire accompanied by the appearance of one as the Son of God, who, we believe, was Jesus Christ.

We might ask, "Where was Daniel?" Might this be an analogy of the tribulation, where the Church (Daniel) is removed before and Israel (Daniel's companions) is preserved through troubling times.

Handwriting on the Wall
Daniel 5

Baltasar's Feast by Domenico Fiasella (17th century)

Belshazzar, king of Babylon, used the vessels, plundered from Israel's temple to host a feast, during which a divine hand, that we presume was Christ's, appeared along the wall and wrote a message to the king. His advisors could not decipher it, so he called Daniel, promising advancement and gifts. Daniel rejected both and read:

MENE, MENE, TEKEL, and PARSIN. This is the interpretation of the matter: MENE, God has numbered the days of your kingdom and brought it to an end. TEKEL, you have been weighed in the balances and found wanting. PERES, your kingdom is divided and given to the Medes and Persians.

That very night, Belshazzar the Chaldean king was killed...

Daniel in the Lions' Den
Daniel 6

Daniel in the Lions' Den by Peter Paul Rubens (1614-1616)

Daniel was unjustly sentenced to death and miraculously rescued. Christ was unjustly sentenced to death and resurrected.

Endtime Prophecy
Daniel 9

The Prophet Daniel by Michelangelo (1508-1512)

Gabriel to Daniel, *"Seventy 'sevens' are decreed for your people and your holy city to finish transgression, to put an end to sin, to atone for wickedness, to bring in everlasting righteousness, to seal up vision and prophecy and to anoint the Most Holy Place."*

"Know and understand this: From the time the word goes out to restore and rebuild Jerusalem until the Anointed One, the ruler, comes, there will be seven 'sevens,' and sixty-two 'sevens.' It will be rebuilt with streets and a trench, but in times of trouble. After the sixty-two 'sevens' the Anointed One will be put to death and will have nothing."

"The people of the ruler who will come will destroy the city and the sanctuary. The end will come like a flood: War will continue until the end, and desolations have been decreed. He will confirm a covenant with many for one 'seven.' In the middle of the 'seven' he will put an end to sacrifice and offering. And at the temple he will set up an abomination that causes desolation, until the end that is decreed is poured out on him."

One calculation contends the command to restore and rebuild Jerusalem came on March 14, 445 BC, 69 weeks (of years), or 173,880 days (using a 360-day prophetic year) later, on April 6, 32 A.D, Jesus rode into Jerusalem on a donkey proclaiming Himself the Anointed One. He was crucified later that week on Passover and rose on Firstfruits.

The Romans subsequently destroyed Jerusalem in 70 A.D. The remainder of the prophecy, the final week, is awaiting fulfillment.

Return
Ezra 1

King Cyrus Handing over the Treasure Looted from the Temple of Jerusalem by Ferdinand Bol (1660-1663)

"Thus says Cyrus king of Persia: The Lord, the God of heaven, has given me all the kingdoms of the earth, and He has charged me to build Him a house at Jerusalem, which is in Judah. Whoever is among you of all His people, may his God be with him, and let him go up to Jerusalem, which is in Judah, and rebuild the house of the Lord, the God of Israel—He is the God who is in Jerusalem. And let each survivor, in whatever place he sojourns, be assisted by the men of his place with silver and gold, with goods and with beasts, besides freewill offerings for the house of God that is in Jerusalem."

And why did King Cyrus make such a pronouncement? Some believe Daniel gave him the scroll of Isaiah to read, written 150 years earlier. In Chapter 44 it states: *Thus says the Lord, your Redeemer... Who says of Cyrus, 'He is My shepherd, and he shall fulfill all My purpose'; saying of Jerusalem, 'She shall be built,' and of the temple, 'Your foundation shall be laid.'"*

What would you have done as Cyrus?

Esther

The Festival of Esther by Edward Armitage RA (1865)

Haman, King Ahasuerus' leading official, attempted to eradicate the Jews because of his hatred for Queen Esther's cousin Mordecai. Esther told the King of his plan, and when the king saw Haman prostrate himself before his wife, he thought she was being harassed and ordered Haman hung on the gallows planned for Mordecai, who took Haman's place with Ahasuerus and used that position to save the Jewish people.

Many have tried to eliminated the Hebrew people or the kingly line to the Messiah. They will never succeed. The pattern points to the One who will come save them in the end time, Jesus Christ. They will need to recognize it first. It has been written.

Today the Jews celebrate the joyous holiday of Purim.

Bethlehem
Micah 5

Journey of the Magi with their Retinue by August von Wörndle (1852)

Wise men from the East did indeed go to Bethlehem looking for the new king. It may have had something to do with records Daniel created while leading the Babylonian wise men (Daniel 2), since Daniel knew the timing of His arrival (Daniel 9).

We know they asked King Herod, who pointed to the prophecy of Micah 5, whose writings came before Daniel.

But you, O Bethlehem Ephrathah, who are too little to be among the clans of Judah, from you shall come forth for Me one who is to be ruler in Israel, whose coming forth is from of old, from ancient days.

Gabriel visits Zechariah
Luke 1

The Visit of the Angel to Zechariah by Luis Paret y Alcazar (1786)

Zechariah was serving in the temple as a priest, part of the division of Abijah, when the angel Gabriel told him a son would be born to him named John.

Some use this visitation to date the birth of Jesus Christ to the Feast of Trumpets.

Massacre of the Innocents
Jeremiah 31 - Matthew 2

Massacre of the Innocents by Peter Paul Rubens (1610-11)

When the wise men failed to return to Herod, he had all the male children two-years and younger butchered in Bethlehem. He did not want to relinquish his throne. Mary and Joseph had already fled to Egypt with Jesus following an angel's warning.

Matthew records this as a fulfillment of Jeremiah 31:

Thus, says the Lord: "A voice is heard in Ramah, lamentation and bitter weeping. Rachel is weeping for her children; she refuses to be comforted for her children, because they are no more."

Ramah, near Bethlehem, is the burial site of Rachel, weeping in her tomb, for the butchery of these innocents.

Out of Egypt I called My Son
Hosea 11/13 – Matthew 1

The Flight into Egypt by Peter Paul Rubens (1577-1640)

Hosea wrote... *When Israel was a child, I loved him, and out of Egypt I called my son...* clearly a reference to the exodus led by Moses.

Over 800 years later, after finding the Christ Child in Bethlehem, the wise men were warned not to return to Herod, who sought to kill the Child. An angel appeared to Joseph in a dream, warning him to take his family and flee to Egypt until he was called.

That call came upon Herod's death. Joseph chose to settle in Nazareth because Herod's son, Archelaus, was reigning in Judea. God's only begotten Son was called out of Egypt.

Hosea went on to speak for the Lord to Israel, *But I am the LORD your God from the land of Egypt; you know no God but Me, and besides Me there is no savior.*

Vision of Four Chariots
Zechariah 6

The Vision of the Four Chariots by Gustave Doré (1832-1883)

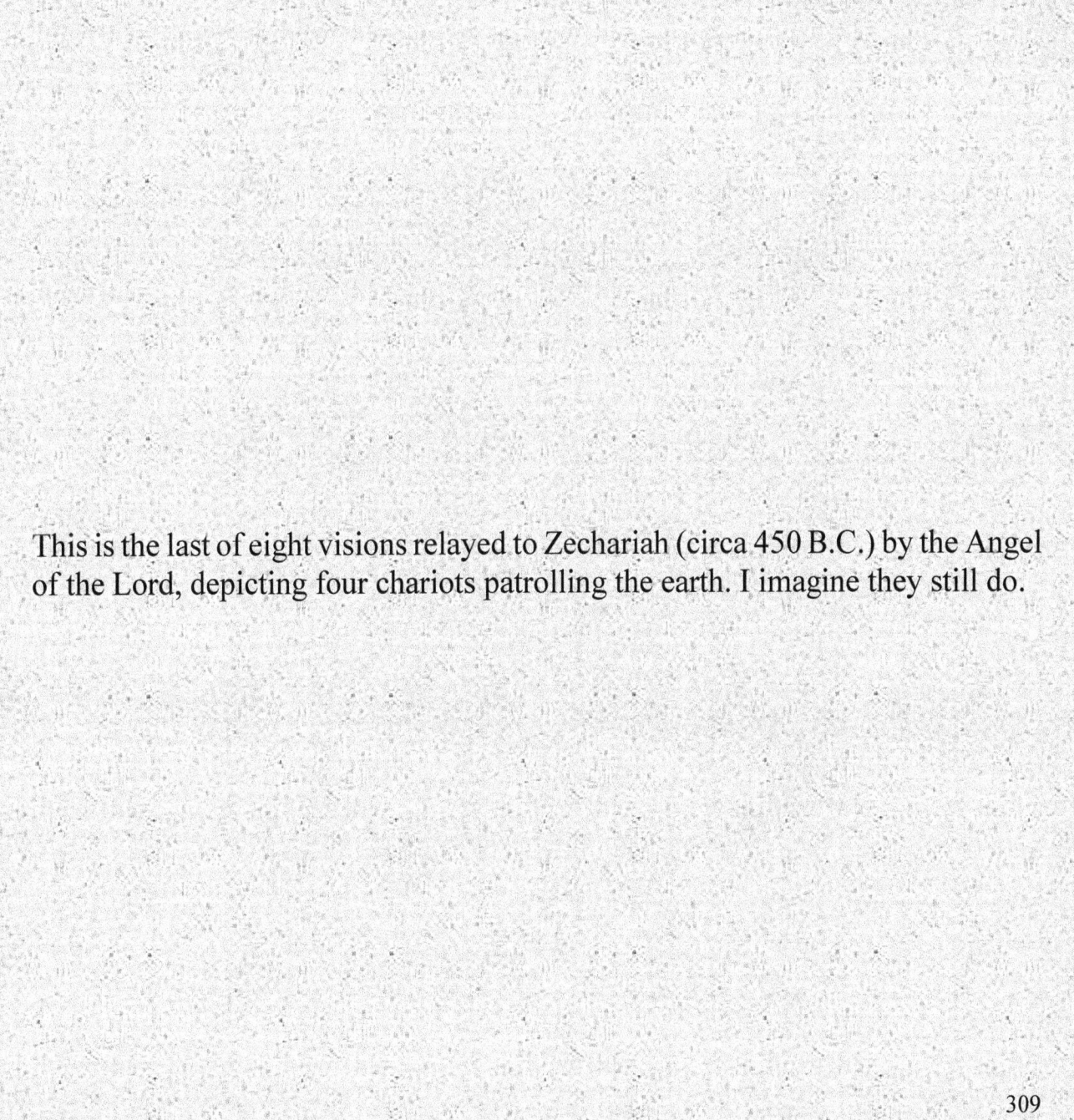

This is the last of eight visions relayed to Zechariah (circa 450 B.C.) by the Angel of the Lord, depicting four chariots patrolling the earth. I imagine they still do.

He is Coming
Malachi 3 – Matthew 3

St. John the Baptist Preaching by Mattia Preti (1665)

Behold, I send My messenger, and he will prepare the way before Me. And the Lord whom you seek will suddenly come to His temple; and the messenger of the covenant in whom you delight, behold, he is coming, says the Lord of hosts.

Five centuries later…

In those days John the Baptist came preaching in the wilderness of Judea, "Repent, for the kingdom of heaven is at hand." For this is he who was spoken of by the prophet Isaiah when he said, "The voice of one crying in the wilderness: 'Prepare the way of the Lord; make His paths straight.'"

John the Baptist preparing the way for Jesus Christ.

Feast of Tabernacles
Leviticus 23

Jesus Walks in the Portico of Solomon by James Jacques Joseph Tissot (1886-1894)

There came a time when Jesus lingered in Galilee because the Jews in Judea sought to kill Him. Even His brothers did not believe in Him. When the Feast of Tabernacles (or Booths) was near, they egged Him to go openly to Judea to show His disciples His works. He indicated He did not intend to go, but when they left, He went privately to Jerusalem to teach. (John 7)

This eight-day Feast of the Lord was established in the Old Testament. The Israelites were to build booths and dwell in them for seven days to remind them of the Exodus.

There is a deeper meaning of the feast. God came to <u>tabernacle</u>, or live, with us in human form. His chosen people rejected Him, but He will return in time, when they are ready.

The King Riding a Donkey
Zechariah 9 – John 12

Entry of Christ into Jerusalem by Anthony van Dyck (1599-1641)

In His last week, Jesus entered Jerusalem riding a donkey; Zechariah's prophecy:

Rejoice greatly, Daughter Zion! Shout, Daughter Jerusalem! See, your King comes to you, righteous and victorious, lowly and riding on a donkey, on a colt, the foal of a donkey.

Unleavened Bread
Leviticus 23

The Communion of the Apostles by James Jacques Joseph Tissot (1886-1894)

Unleavened bread is eaten at all Passover meals because the seven-day Feast of Unleavened Bread begins the day after Passover and was mandated by God.

Seven days you shall eat unleavened bread. On the first day, you shall remove leaven out of your houses, for if anyone eats what is leavened, from the first day until the seventh day, that person shall be cut off from Israel. (Exodus 12)

Why unleavened bread?

Leaven in the Old Testament is a symbol of sin because it puffs up.

But Jesus was free of sin, which is why death could not hold Him, and He rose on the Feast of Firstfruits.

Requirement for Return
Hosea 5 - Acts 1

The Ascension of the Lord by Francisco Bayeu y Subías (1769)

When Jesus left Earth, the (angels) standing with the apostles told them He would return in the same way (Acts 1).

There is, some think, a prerequisite found in Hosea 5:

I will return again to My place, until they acknowledge their guilt and seek My face, and in their distress earnestly seek Me.

Perhaps their guilt was rejecting the Messiah, though they won't understand until they are immensely oppressed, perhaps the holocaust of Zechariah 13.

The Great Day of the Lord's Wrath
Zechariah 14

The Great Day of His Wrath by John Martin (1851-1853)

Scripture is not just the history of mankind and the selection of the Hebrews as the Lord's chosen people, the light unto the nations (Isaiah 42:6), the generational line of the Messiah, Jesus Christ, who is the light of the world, but it specifies events, beginning to end, and details a time in the not-too-distant future, we think, where the stubbornness of the hearts of men reaches a point where the Lord returns to set things right.

Behold, a day is coming for the Lord, when the spoil taken from you will be divided in your midst. For I will gather all the nations against Jerusalem to battle... Then the Lord will go out and fight against those nations as when He fights on a day of battle. On that day His feet shall stand on the Mount of Olives that lies before Jerusalem on the east, and the Mount of Olives shall be split in two from east to west by a very wide valley, so that one half of the Mount shall move northward, and the other half southward. And you shall flee... then the Lord my God will come, and all the holy ones with Him... And the Lord will be King over all the earth.

This will be the second coming of our Lord Jesus Christ, whose feet alight on the Mount of Olives, and He shall become Lord and King over all the earth.

Meaning behind the letters

Hebrew Alphabet

Print	Final	Paleo	Ancient	Letter	Pronunciation	Value	Basic Meaning
א		₭	𐤀	Aleph	Silent letter	1	GOD, Creator, first, strength, leader, LORD, King, sovereign
ב		꒕	ﻼ	Bet / Vet	B as in Bethlehem / V as in Vine	2	house, temple, tabernacle, in, tent, body, dwelling, universe
ג		∧	ᒋ	Gimmel	G as in Give	3	to lift up
ד		◁	ᛘ	Dalet	D as in Door	4	door, path
ה		⊒	⚓	Hey	H as in House	5	reveal, show, behold, grace, mercy, what comes from, spirit
ו		Y	Y	Vav / Waw	V as in Vine / W as in Wine	6	join, nail, secure, establish, man
ז		I	𐤆	Zayin	Z as in Zion	7	cut, pierce, weapon
ח		⊟	ⅲ	Chet	CH as in BaCH	8	fence, inner chamber, gate, separate, protect
ט		⊗	⊗	Tet	T as in Tall	9	surrounds, twists
י		⟲	⌐	Yod	Y as in Yes	10	work, hand, activity, deed
כ	ך	⼂	⨆	Kaf	K as in King / CH as in BaCH	20	open, cover, give, close, crowning accomplishment
ל		⌒	⌒	Lamed	L as in Levi	30	rod, authority, tongue, teaching
מ	ם	⒒	⋎	Mem	M as in Mother	40	water, chaos, disorder, strength, mighty, Messiah
נ	ן	ㄣ	⌇	Nun	N as in Now	50	life, activity, action
ס		≢	⌁	Samech	S as in sun	60	support, turning aside, twisting, protection
ע		○	⊙	Ayin	Silent letter	70	eye, see, understand, insight perceive
פ	ף	⌐	⊖	Pey	P as in People / F as in Fast	80	mouth, speak, open
צ	ץ	⌐	⌐	Tsade	TS as in BaTS	90	To pull, a hook, desire, harvest
ק		⌐	⊖	Qof	K as in King	100	what is final, what is behind, last, least, final, future
ר		◁	⌐	Resh	R as in Royal	200	highest, most important, person
ש		W	⊔⊔	Shin	SH as in Shape / S as in Sun	300	consume, destroy
ת		×	†	Tav	T as in Time	400	cross, covenant, truth, perfection, sign, ownership, seal

Copyright 1996-2016 For HIS Glory All Rights Reserved

Historians believe Ancient Hebrew was the way the language was originally written, meaning in pictographic form. Every letter bears some meaning, based on its shape and usage.

Father, for example, is Alef-Beyt, meaning leader of the house.

If you add a Hey in the middle, you get the word love. Hey seems to have a spiritual flavor, after all, we believe God is love (1 John 4:16). God changed Sarai and Abram's names by adding a Hey. (Genesis 17)

Now the name of God, Yahweh, is found first in Exodus 3 and seen nearly 7,000 times in scripture. Hebrew is written right to left, and Yahweh is spelled Yod-Hey-Vav-Hey. If you read the name left to right, as we do in English, the meaning reads behold the nail, behold the hand.

How did they know?

The Road to Emmaus
Luke 24

Road to Emmaus by Robert Zund (1877)

The volume of the book (Psalm 40 and Hebrews 10) speaks of Jesus. After He arose, He journeyed with two of His disciples, one of whom was Cleopas, on the road to Emmaus. The disciples did not recognize Him. Some think His beard had been ripped off (Isaiah 50), and as they spoke about what had recently happened, this being the third day after the crucifixion, Jesus explained, beginning with Moses and all the prophets, the things concerning Himself.

Shroud of Turin
Midjourney AI Generated

Daily Express/Midjourney (2024)

What did Jesus really look like? Portraits of Him are strikingly similar. Might this be based on some truth?

The Shroud of Turin is a famous relic, a three-dimensional image of a crucified man embedded in linen, first appearing in historical records around 1354 A.D. in France, and claimed to be the burial cloth of Christ.

One of the most studied artifacts in history, scientists reveal the cloth may very well date back two thousand years to the time of the crucifixion.

One day we will ask Him.

Indwelling Spirit
Acts 2

Pentecost by Joseph Ignaz Mildorfer (1719-1775)

The Lord physically talked to many people in the Old Testament. That physical aspect we see as the preincarnate appearance of Jesus Christ.

The Lord is intimately involved in every aspect of life. Paul said *in Him we live, and move, and have our being.* (Acts 17)

At Pentecost (circa 32 A.D.), which falls on the fourth of the Lord's seven Feasts, Jesus sent the Holy Spirit to indwell those who believe in Him, then you hear from Him directly through your conscience.

Jesus said… *If any man thirst, let him come unto me, and drink. He that believes on me, as the scripture has said, out of his belly shall flow rivers of living water.* (John 7)

The Volume of the Book is about Him.

May the Lord richly bless us.

Illustrations and Art

Cover: Christ by Emily Tjonmsland (2024) – Used with permission
Christ and the Penitent Sinners by Pieter Paul Rubens (1618)
The Ancient of Days by William Blake (1794)
Saint John the Evangelist by Bernardo Cavallino (1616-1656)
Paul Writing His Epistles by Valentin de Boulogne (1620)
Adam Naming the Animals by Jan Brueghel the Younger (17th century)
The Lord with Adam and Eve in the Garden of Eden by Jacob de Backer (1559)
Adam and Eve's Original Sin by Raphaël (1519)
The Expulsion of Adam and Eve from Paradise by Benjamin West (1791)
The Sacrifice of Abel by Arsène Robert (1870)
Cain and Able by Pietro Novelli (1603-1647)
God Took Enoch by Gerard Hoet (1648-1733)
Birth of Noah by James Tissot (1896-1902)
The Sons of God Saw the Daughters of Men That They Were Fair by Maurice Greiffenhagen (1862-1931)
Noah, The Eve of the Deluge by John Linnell (1848)
The Animals Entering the Ark by Giovanni Francesco Castiglione (1641-1710)
Noah in the Ark by Ditlev Blunck (1835)
Sacrifice of Noah by Pacecco de Rosa (1607-1657)
Noah's Thanks Offering by Joseph Anton Koch (1803)
The Building of the Tower of Babel by Marten van Valckenborch I (1534–1612)
Abraham's Journey from Ur to Canaan by József Molnár (1850)
The Meeting of Abraham and Melchizedek by Peter Paul Rubens (1626)
A Deep Sleep Fell Upon Abram is an illustration from the 1728 *Figures de la Bible* Illustrated by Gerard Hoet (1648–1733) and others
Hagar and the Angel by Giuseppe Bottani (1717 – 1784)

Circumcision of Jesus by Niccolò Pallavicino (1605) (originally done by Peter Paul Rubens in 1577)
Abraham Receiving the Three Angeles by Bartolome Esteban Murillo (1667)
Sodom and Gomorrah by John Martin (1852)
Abraham is summoned before Abimelech; Sarah is given back to Abraham by Nicolaes Berchem (1670)
The Angel of the Lord Preventing Abraham from Sacrificing his Son Isaac by Pieter Lastman (1616)
Rebecca and Eliezer by Alexandre Cabanel (1883)
Plate with the coat of arms of Isabelle d'Este-Gonzague, Marchioness of Mantua, with decoration of Abimelech spying on Isaac and Rebecca by Nicholas of Urbino (1524-1525)
Isaac Blessing Jacob by Matthias Stom (1635)
Jacob's Dream by Luther Terry (1852)
Jacob's Departure from Laban by Luca Giordano (1705)
Jacob Wrestling with the Angel by Alexander Louis Leloir (1865)
Meeting between Esau and Jacob Giovanni Maria Bottala (1636-1641)
Rape of Dinah by Guiliano Bugiardini (15th-16th century)
The Death of Rachel by Gustav Metz (1847)
Joseph Reveals His Dream to His Brethren by James Jacques Joseph Tissot (1896-1902)
Joseph Sold by His Brothers by Giovanni Maria Bottala (1636-1642)
Jacob Mourns His Son Joseph by James Jacques Joseph Tissot (1896-1902)
Judah and Tamar by Ferdinand Bol (1644)
Joseph and Potiphar's Wife by Guido Reni (1630)
Joseph Interprets the Dreams While in Prison by James Jacques Joseph Tissot (1896-1902)
Joseph Receiving Pharaoh's Ring by Giovanni Battista Tiepolo (1733-1735)
Joseph Recognized by His Brothers by Jean-Charles Tardieu (1788)

Jacob Blessing Ephraim and Manasseh, by Benjamin West (1766-1768)
The Death of Jacob by Pietro Benvenuti (1769-1844)
Job and His Friends by Ilya Repin (1869)
Moses Saved from the River by Nicolas Poussin (1638)
Moses and the Daughters of Jethro by Ciro Ferri (1633-1689)
Burning Bush by Sébastien Bourdon (17th century)
The Plague of Flies by James Jacques Joseph Tissot (1896-1902)
And There Was a Great Cry in Egypt by Arthur Hacker (1897)
Lamentations over the Death of the First-Born of Egypt by Charles Sprague Pearce (1877)
The Israelites Crossing the Desert by William West (1845)
Crossing the Red Sea by Luca Giordano (1681)
Song of Miriam the Prophetess by Luca Giordano (1687)
The Israelites Gathering the Manna in the Desert by Nicolas Poussin (1637-1639)
Moses and Aaron Speak to the People by James Jacques Joseph Tissot (1896-1902)
The Grapes of Canaan by James Jacques Joseph Tissot (1896-1902)
Moses Striking the Rock by Nicolas Poussin (1649)
Praying Moses with Aaron and Hur on Mount Horeb by Joseph von Führich (1832)
Moses Receives the Tablets of the Law by João Zeferino da Costa (1868)
Moses and the Golden Calf by Domenico Gargiulo (1609-1675)
The Israelites' Encampment in the Wilderness, Guided by God by J. J. Derghi (1866)
Moses and Joshua Before the Tabernacle by James Jacques Joseph Tissot (1896-1902)
Moses and the Brazen Serpent by Peter Paul Rubens (1610)
Landscape with Balaam by Joseph Anton Koch (1832-1836)
Phinehas Slaying Zimri and Kozbi the Midianite by Jeremias van Winghe (1585-1645)
The Dead Bodies Carried Away by James Jacques Joseph Tissot (1896-1902)
The Daughters of Zelophehad, Illustration from The Bible and Its Story Taught by One Thousand Picture Lessons. Edited by Charles F. Horne and Julius A. Bewer (1908)
The City of Refuge by George Tinworth for Doulton & Co (2007)

Aspergillum as Described in Leviticus by Julia O'Gara (2011)
Sacrifice of Moses by Massimo Stanzione (1650) Italian Wikipedia
The Scapegoat by William Holman Hunt (1854-1855)
The Death of Moses by Musée Fabre (1850)
Rahab and the Emissaries of Joshua (17th century, artist unknown)
The Captain of the Lord's Army Appears to Joshua by Ferdinand Bol (1616-1680) - Public Domain rijksmuseum.nl/
The Seven Trumpets of Jericho by James Jacques Joseph Tissot (1896-1902)
Joshua Stops the Rotation of the Sun by Carlo Maratta (1700)
Hall of Justice fresco, Ehud Kills Eglon king of the Moabites by Teofilo Torri (1608)
Jael Shows to Barak, Sisera Lying Dead by James Jacques Joseph Tissot (1896-1902)
The Angel and Gideon by Gerbrand van den Eeckhout (1640)
Jephthah Returning from Battle is Greeted by his Daughter by Giovanni Antonio Pellegrini (1708-1713)
Sacrifice of Manoah by Pieter Lastman (1624) – Wikipedia
Samson and the Lion by Luca Giordano (1694-1696)
Samson and Delilah by Anthony van Dyck (1599-1641)
Samson Destroys the Philistine Temple by Giovanni Benedetto Castiglione called Grechetto (17th century)
The Levite of Ephraim by Alexandre-François Caminade (1837)
Ruth and Naomi by Philip Hermogenes Calderon (1833-1898)
Ruth in Boaz's Field by Julius Schnorr von Carolsfeld (1828)
Hannah at Prayer by Wilhelm Wachtel (1875-1942)
Depiction of Eli and Samuel by John Singleton Copley (1780)
The Plague of the Philistines at Ashdod by Pieter van Halen (1661)
Saul Reproved by Samuel by John Singleton Copley (1798)
Annointing of David by Samuel by Felix-Joseph Barrias (1842)
David and Saul by Ernst Josephson (1878)
David Slaying Goliath by Peter Paul Rubens (1616)

The Wise Abigail by Luca Giordano (1696-1697)
Saul and the Witch of Endor by Benjamin West (1777)
Death of King Saul by Elie Zvi Marcuse (1850)
David Bearing the Ark of Testament into Jerusalem by Domenico Gargiulo (1609-1675)
The Prophet Nathan Rebukes King David by Eugène Siberdt (1866-1931)
Appearance of the Angel to King David by Luca Giordano (-1705)
Christ on the Cross between the Two by Peter Paul Rubens (1620)
Solomon's Dream by Luca Giordano (1693)
The Death of Absalom woven in 1817 at the Royal Tapestry Factory in Madrid, under the guidance of its director, Don Livinio Stuyck y Vandergoten
Bathsheba's Appeal to David by Govert Flinck (1651)
The Judgement of Solomon by Mattias Stom (1640) – Wikipedia
The Queen of Sheba before the temple of Solomon in Jerusalem by Salomon de Bray (1597-1664)
Vanity of Vanities and All is Vanity by Isaac Asknaziy (19th Century)
The Shunamite Relating the Glories of King Solomon to her Maidens by Albert Joseph Moore (1894)
King Solomon's Idolatry by Giovanni Venanzi di Pesaro (1668)
Jeroboam Offering Sacrifice for the Idol by Jean-Honoré Fragonard (1752)
Jeroboam's Wife and Prophet Ahija by Ludovico Venuti (1822)
Elijah Raises the Widow's Son by Benjamin West. Colorized by Valentine Green (1799)
The Sacrifice of Elijah Before the Priests of Baal by Domenico Fetti (1621-1622)
Elijah Running in Front of King Ahab's Chariot Towards Jezreel by Jean-Baptiste Despax (1710-1773)
An Angel Awakens the Prophet Elijah by Juan Antonio Frias y Escalante (1667)
Jezebel by Harold Copping (1863-1932)
Elijah Taken Up in a Chariot of Fire by Giuseppe Angeli (1740)

Elisha Dividing the Waters of Jordan with Elijah's Mantle by Jean-Baptiste Despax (1710-1773)
The Prophet Elisha by Giorgio Vasari (1566)
Elisha Refuses the Gifts of Namaan by Ferdinand Bol (1661)
Proclaiming Joash King by Edward Bird RA (1815)
The Miracle at the Grave of Elisha by Jan Nagel (1596)
Adoration of the Shepherds by Gerard van Honthorst (1622)
The Fallen Angel by Alexandre Cabanel (1847)
The Destruction of Leviathan from Doré's English Bible (1866)
Christ Healing the Blind Man by Gioacchino Assereto (1640)
He Heals the Lame by James Jacques Joseph Tissot (1886-1894)
Battle of Sennacherib by Tanzio da Varallo (1629-1630)
God the Father and the Holy Spirit by Pompeo Batoni (1740-1743)
Jesus Unrolls the Book in the Synagogue by James Jacques Joseph Tissot (1886 – 1894) - Wikiart
King Manasseh in Exile by Maarten de Vos (1603)
The Death of King Josiah by Antonio Zanchi (1660)
The Prophet Jeremiah Prophesies the Fall of Jerusalem to King Zedekiah by Joseph Stallaert (1825-1903)
The Flight of the Prisoners by James Jacques Joseph Tissot (1896-1902)
Jonah and the Whale by Pieter Lastman (1621)
Jonah Under His Gourd by Maarten van Heemskerck (1561)
The Vision of the Prophet Ezekiel by Ditlev Blunck (1830)
The Vision of Ezekiel by Francisco Collantes (1630)
God's Judgment upon Gog by Asher Brown Durand (1851-1852)
Daniel before Nebuchadnezzar by Salomon (de) Koninck (1609–1656)
Shadrach, Meshach and Abednego in the Furnace by Luca Giordano (1705)
Baltasar's Feast by Domenico Fiasella (17th century)
Daniel in the Lions' Den by Peter Paul Rubens (1614-1616)

The Prophet Daniel by Michelangelo (1508-1512)
King Cyrus Handing over the Treasure Looted from the Temple of Jerusalem by Ferdinand Bol (1660-1663)
The Festival of Esther by Edward Armitage RA (1865)
Journey of the Magi with their Retinue by August von Wörndle (1852)
The Visit of the Angel to Zechariah by Luis Paret y Alcazar (1786)
Massacre of the Innocents by Peter Paul Rubens (1610-11)
The Flight into Egypt by Peter Paul Rubens (1577-1640)
The Vision of the Four Chariots by Gustave Doré (1832-1883)
St. John the Baptist Preaching by Mattia Preti (1665)
Jesus Walks in the Portico of Solomon by James Jacques Joseph Tissot (1886-1894)
Entry of Christ into Jerusalem by Anthony van Dyck (1599-1641)
The Communion of the Apostles by James Jacques Joseph Tissot (1886-1894)
The Ascension of the Lord by Francisco Bayeu y Subías (1769)
The Great Day of His Wrath by John Martin (1851-1853)
Ancient Hebrew Alphabet – public domain
Road to Emmaus by Robert Zund (1877)
Shroud of Turin AI Midjourney generated image by Daily Express (2024)
Pentecost by Joseph Ignaz Mildorfer (1719-1775)
Christ by Emily Tjonmsland (2024) – Used with permission
From Wikimedia unless noted

The Volume of the Book
Genesis - Malachi

Christ by Emily Tjonmsland (2024)

Author

Commander George J Thielemann (USN, Ret) and his wife Telli

BA Psychology University of Wisconsin (Madison), MAT Education Northwestern University, MA National Security Naval War College USN service 1976-2005, including Naval Flight Officer hunting Russian submarines from P3C aircraft, ASWOC Director Keflavik Iceland, Officer Candidate School Director, USAF Academy Assistant Professor of Political Science, CCG-7 N6 overseeing afloat Naval Force communications in the Arabian Sea for Afghan Operation Enduring Freedom after 9/11. Elementary School Teacher 1973-1976 and 2005-2019, Peace Corps Thailand volunteer until Covid shutdown worldwide 2020. Lifelong Biblical scholar. Both George and Telli are cancer survivors, and volunteer for various organizations, including Hospice.

Editor

Pastor Charlie Garrett and his wife Hideko

Charlie attended Southern Evangelical Seminary and Bible College and graduated Magna Cum Laude in 2009. He was ordained at Grace Baptist Church, Sarasota in 2010, and pastors The Superior Word Church which airs his teachings online. He has written an analysis of every verse in the Bible from Romans 1:1 to Revelation 22:11. His sermons include detailed studies in Hebrew and Greek as well as the cultural, historical, and pictorial aspects of the text presented. Charlie has been married to his wife, Hideko, for 41 years. They have two grown children and a house full of Chihuahuas.

Reviewed by Carol Thompson for Readers' Favorite
Review Rating: 5 Stars
19 April, 2025

The Volume of the Book is a richly illustrated and deeply devotional study tracing the presence of Jesus Christ throughout the Old Testament. With a clear emphasis on typology and biblical foreshadowing, the work presents a Christ-centered interpretation of Scripture that highlights the unity of the Bible from Genesis through the early historical books. The book includes biblical passages, traditional interpretations, and classic works of art to show how Christ is the central figure of the biblical narrative, even in texts written centuries before His incarnation. Every chapter reflects on a fundamental narrative or figure from the Old Testament and clarifies its importance to Christ's identity and redemptive purpose. The stories of Isaac's sacrifice, the Passover lamb, the bronze serpent in the wilderness, and the manna from heaven are all examined as early foreshadowings of Jesus' life, death, and resurrection. Additionally, the arrangement of the Tabernacle and the practices of the Levitical priesthood are analyzed from this Christological perspective.

The author does not seek to provide academic analysis or historical critique. Rather, he encourages readers to reflect on Scripture as a cohesive revelation that directs us to the Messiah. The tone is both devotional and respectful, and the combination of Scripture with classical art enhances this contemplative narrative. The artwork is remarkable; with many pieces I had never encountered before. Ideal for Christians seeking a theologically immersive yet accessible study, The Volume of the Book is a scriptural journey and a spiritual affirmation of Christ's presence throughout the Old Testament. It encourages a deeper appreciation for the consistency of God's redemptive plan and the centrality of Jesus from beginning to end. It's very well written, and I highly recommend it.

www.ingramcontent.com/pod-product-compliance
Lightning Source LLC
Chambersburg PA
CBHW061348010526
44107CB00011B/871